Bank Notes

Series editor **David Palfreman**
Senior Lecturer,
Central Manchester College

This series provides a structured revision programme for students taking their Institute of Bankers Stage 2 Banking Diploma examinations.

By answering a series of Short Answer Tests at the front of the book, students can decide on their revision priorities. Taking one topic at a time, they can refresh their knowledge of the topic using the Study Guide, and then test themselves using the Multiple Choice Questions. Most importantly, detailed notes on *all* answers to the Multiple Choice Questions are given, so that students can reinforce their learning by discovering why wrong answers *are* wrong.

Finally, by tackling the Post-tests for each topic, students can test the effectiveness of their revision.

There are eight titles in the series:

Law Relating to Banking
Monetary Economics
Accountancy
Investment
Nature of Management
Finance of International Trade
Practice of Banking 1
Practice of Banking 2

INSTITUTE OF BANKERS
STAGE 2 BANKING DIPLOMA

Nature of Management

B W STONE

VNR
UK Van Nostrand Reinhold (UK) Co. Ltd

First published in 1987 by
Van Nostrand Reinhold (UK) Co. Ltd
Molly Millars Lane, Wokingham, Berkshire,
England

Typeset in Ehrhardt 10 on 11½ point by
Columns Ltd, Reading

Printed and bound in Great Britain by
Billing & Sons Ltd, Worcester

ISBN 0 278 00000 2

*I'd like to acknowledge the friendship of my
Resident Dramatic Vegetarian and of my
Favourite Urban Peasant, whose copings with
the Examination System spurred me to keep
writing this book.*

Contents

Editor's Introduction

What's this book about?

This book will help you pass your Institute of Bankers examination.
Interested? Well, read on and you'll see how.

You're probably at the stage in your studies when you've got information coming out of your ears, a huge file of notes and the exam looming ever nearer! Quite possibly, you're beginning to get that familiar feeling of desperation: 'Where do I start?', 'I'll never learn all this.'

Help is at hand. If you use this book properly you'll discover where you should start and you'll learn more efficiently. Perhaps this will be the first time you'll have approached study in a methodical, effective fashion. By the way, we won't be throwing a whole lot of new information at you — you probably know quite enough already; there's nothing in this book which you shouldn't already know or, perhaps, knew once but have forgotten! Our aim is to help you understand, learn and use it.

So you want to pass the exam...

Well, your study should be: *positive, efficient,* and *effective.* Remember two *key ideas:*
— *Organization*
— *Activity*

Organization

Let's explain what we mean. *How well organized are you?* Do you waste time looking for things, do you spend as long getting ready to do something as actually doing it? How many times have we seen students ploughing through a thoroughly disorganized file to find something? What a waste of time! The point is made, we think; so get yourself organized.

Time: When are you going to study? Only you know when you've the time and only you know when you work best. For example, are you a 'lark' or an 'owl'? Be realistic. It's no good trying to revise for a few minutes here and there, while the adverts are on, for example. You must commit a *realistic* amount of time to any one session — probably not less than one hour and not more than three.

Have you ever thought of formally timetabling your study? Look at the timetable shown. You could draw similar ones (one for each week) and mark in your revision times.

As you can see, the timetable caters for both 'larks' and 'owls', as well as for all tendencies in between. Clearly there'll be major blocks of time when you can't do any study — you have to go to work — but that still leaves a lot of available time. Make the best use of it. A word of warning, however: if you have long-standing or important domestic or leisure commitments, think twice about breaking them. At least try first to build them into your timetable.

Study Timetable

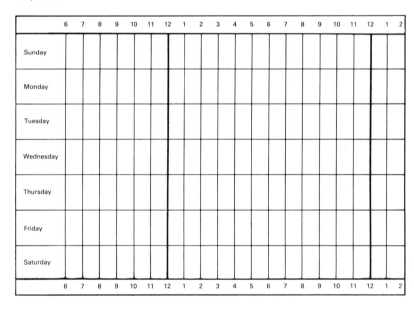

Place: The kitchen table or the sofa in front of the TV are *not* the ideal places to work. You need to be able to concentrate and this means finding somewhere *reasonably quiet* — don't try to revise with the Hi-Fi on! Equally important you need somewhere which is *comfortable*: a good chair, a desk or table, and good lighting. Ideally, you should be able to leave your work out, ready to come back to, so that you don't waste time at the start of your next session — one reason why the kitchen table isn't suitable.

Pace: Contrary to popular practice, it's *not* a good idea to leave revision to the last minute, particularly if you want to revise positively, efficiently and effectively.

Plan your revision: We've included some short answer tests which you should complete before reading the rest of the book. These exercises will help you identify your own strengths and weaknesses and so help you to determine how long you need to spend on each topic.

Use your study timetable to plan a revision campaign. Believe me, the more carefully you plan, the more you'll get done in any given time. Of course, you're bound to end up working like crazy for the few days immediately before the exam, so you might as well plan for this as well! What must not happen, and a planned revision campaign will prevent this, is finding that you haven't allocated your time properly and that there's just no way you're going to be able to study everything thoroughly in time.

Activity

How long can you concentrate on any one thing? If you're honest, not very long. And when it comes to revision, let's face it, it really takes the prize in the boredom stakes. No one likes to just sit there trying to learn something. But don't despair — there are ways to make it more bearable and effective. Read on.

What you should not do is sit there reading the same original notes over and over again. It's not only excruciatingly boring, it's also very unproductive. After you've read your notes through once, you'll find you know much of what you're reading already and progressively more of your time will be wasted each time you repeat the exercise.

Bank Notes: *Be active*, and this is where the *Bank Notes* series comes into its own. If you use each book properly (see *How to use this book* on p. xv) you'll find yourself very active in your study. In particular, you'll be interacting with the subject matter instead of being a passive, and not particularly absorbant, sponge.

Your aims: Remember, however, that this series is not a substitute for your own hard work; you'll still have to put in *time* and *effort*. Your study should have three aims:
— Complete *understanding* of the topic.
— *Retention* and *recall* of it.
— The ability to *explain* and *apply* what you have learnt.

Study activities: So, a few general suggestions for *study activities*, all tried and tested, to achieve these aims. You'll find further ideas and guidance in the Study Guides to the Topics.

Revision notes: Your course notes and text books are not particularly suitable to revise from. Making revision notes is a good investment of your time. They can consist of just the headings in your notes/text book with, perhaps, a brief note about important principles or unusual points.

Do take care in the way you lay out your notes. Don't try to economize on paper; it's probably the lowest of your overheads anyway! Your notes should look 'attractive' and be easy to follow. Allow space to add other brief comments later. Try the following as a model:

MAIN HEADING
    SUB-HEADING
....

     Sub-sub-Heading
     ....

      1. Important point...
      ....
      2. Important point...
      ....

When you've made your revision notes, you can use them in the following way. Take each note in turn and try to recall and explain the subject matter. If you can, go on to the next; if you can't, look back to your notes/text book — perhaps noting a page number for future reference. By doing this, you'll revise, test your knowledge and generally spend your time productively by concentrating your revision on those aspects of the subject with which you're least familiar. In addition, you'll have an excellent last-minute revision aid.

Summary diagrams: These could be alternatives or additions to revision notes. Many people respond well to diagrammatic explanations and summaries; in particular, the visual association of the different aspects of a subject is useful.

We've two specific types of diagrams in mind: the 'family tree' type and the 'molecule' type, as you'll see below. Of course, if you've seen or can devise other types, use those as well.

Constructing diagrams is a particularly useful form of active study because you have to think how best to construct them and in so doing you'll find you better understand the subject. As with revision notes, don't include too much on each diagram and don't economise on paper. The impact and usefulness of a diagram depends very much on its visual simplicity.

You can use summary diagrams in much the same way as revision notes.

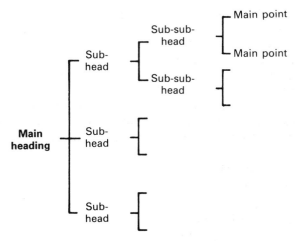

'Family tree' summary diagram (can be constructed vertically or horizontally, as here).

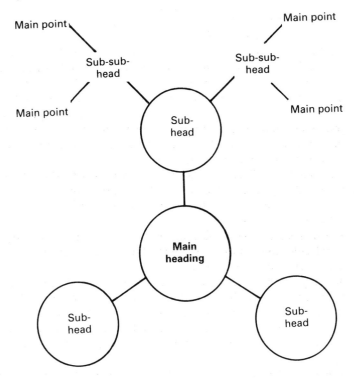

'Molecule' summary diagram.

Useful definitions and explanations: Each subject has a handful of points that are almost certain to come up in at least one question in the exam. So, why not prepare for them? (The *Study Guides* will suggest what these could be.) In practical terms, you may save yourself two or three minutes on each question simply because you don't have to think about how to define or explain something which you probably know well but cannot easily put into words there and then. Multiplied five times, those two or three minutes represent a considerable time saving. We've all wished for another 10–15 minutes in an exam before now!

Plan answers to past questions: Plan them, don't answer them fully. Once you've planned an answer, the writing out is largely a mechanical exercise. If, however, you feel you need the practice, answer some fully.

Examination technique

At this stage in your studies, there's not much we can say to give you a better answering technique. However, there are a number of general points you should remember about actual exam technique.

— *Read the instructions carefully*. You get no extra marks for answering an extra question and you automatically lose a proportion of the possible marks by answering too few. Also, answer the right number of questions from each section. Basic points, perhaps, but you would not believe . . .

— *Read all the questions through* and provisionally select which questions to answer. Be careful in your choice; an apparently simple question may have a hidden twist — don't get caught. Similarly, in a multi-part question be sure you can answer all parts and not just the first.

— Everyone suffers from *exam nerves* and these will probably affect you for the first fifteen minutes or so. Consequently, it's often good practice to answer your 'best' question second or third. By that time you'll be thoroughly relaxed and working well.

— *Plan all your answers* — this is absolutely vital.

— *Divide your time more or less equally between questions*. There's no point spending an extra 15 minutes on your best question if it results in a very poor final question.

— *Check through your answers*. If you spend a few minutes doing this at the end of the exam, you can eliminate minor errors and give a final 'polish' to your answers. When allocating your time, allow five minutes for this.

What do I do now?

You may have been fortunate in your studies and have been taught some or all of the techniques outlined above. If you were, you should now be doubly persuaded of their effectiveness. If you weren't, you've already invested your time well because you're virtually guaranteed to perform better in the exam through having used them than you would otherwise have done.

Back to *Bank Notes*, and where they fit in. We've talked about being 'organized' and 'active' and we've given you a sound set of general ideas as a start. *Bank Notes* go further; not only do they provide an organized and active structure for study, they are also your *personal revision tutor*. Now turn to *How to use this Book* on page xv and start your revision campaign.

How to use this book

At any time in your revision campaign is the simple answer, but the earlier the better. Because we've designed the book to identify any weak areas you may have, and suggest positive ideas to help you study and revise, you'll find this book the ideal basis on which to plan that revision campaign. However, it's equally useful just before the exam when some self-assessment and new revision activities may well revive the flagging spirit!

The different sections

You'll find that this book has *five* sections:

— *Editor's Introduction*: a short but very important section which gives you tried and tested advice on how to revise positively, efficiently and effectively. If you haven't read it, go back and read it now and *only then continue with this section.*

— *How to use this Book*: the section you're reading now.

— *Short Answer Tests*: designed to help you identify your strengths and weaknesses in this subject.

— Ten *Topic Sections*: broadly following the order of the Institute's syllabus and containing:
   an overview of and advice on how best to revise each of the topics,
   Multiple choice questions and full explanatory answers Designed both to test and to teach.

— *Post-tests*: designed to help you assess the effectiveness of your revision and identify any remaining weaknesses.

The short answer tests

You start with these; there's one test for each main section of the syllabus. Complete them all before you go on to the *Topic Sections*. Each test is scored out of 20 and we've allocated marks to the questions — usually two marks to each — and explained in the answers how to score. These tests will quickly give you a good idea of how much you know. By filling in the *Score Grid* — you'll find it inside the back cover — you'll be able to compare your knowledge and understanding on the different parts of the syllabus and identify your revision priorities.

Remember what we said about the value of organization? The *Score Grid* provides an effective chart on which not only to identify and order your revision priorities but also to plot the progress of your revision campaign and assess its efficiency. Look at the *Score Grid* now, and then turn back to here.

The topic sections

When you've completed all ten *Short Answer Tests*, filled in the *Score Grid* and determined the order of your revision, you can turn to the *Topic Sections*.

Study Guides: These, if you like, are your personal revision tutor. Each gives you an overview of the topic and a study framework. We indicate the points you really must know and be able to explain and use, and we point out common student mistakes and give advice on how best to tackle each topic. Some sections already contain revision notes and summary diagrams — remember the *Editor's Introduction* — and you can use these as guides for your further work. For example, if you're given a diagram which summarizes the entire topic, you could take each of the sub-sub-headings in that diagram, use them as main headings and produce more detailed diagrams on those particular parts of the topic.

You can also combine these introductions with the more general advice on study we've already given you. So, you should find that the *Study Guides* form the bases for very thorough revision campaigns on the topics.

Multiple-Choice Questions: You've probably answered 'MCQ' tests before. Such questions are an excellent way of testing knowledge and understanding but the feedback from the tutor is usually minimal, often non-existent. You don't usually know why your answer was right or wrong. Here's where the *Bank Notes* series is different.

It's through the MCQs that the books start to *work with you* to remedy your weaknesses in the different topics and reinforce the knowledge and understanding you already have.

For each question we've given you four possible answers; all are plausible and, indeed, all may be partially correct but only one is totally correct. After each question there's a space to put your answer — **a, b, c,** or **d.** You could also briefly write down the reason you chose that answer, just to stop yourself succumbing to the temption of guessing!

When you've finished all the MCQs for a topic, turn to the answers

— they follow immediately — and mark your own answers.

You score two marks for each correct answer. (Keep a note of your score at the end of the test and enter it on the Score Grid.) We don't just tell you whether you're right or wrong in the answers — we give you a full explanation of why. You'll find these explanations very useful; quite probably the 'penny will drop' where it didn't before.

References to other books: At this point in your studies you might feel it's a bit late to start reading text books! You've probably had enough of them anyway. However, if you consider that you need to do some more reading on a particular point you'll find the books listed below useful. Sometimes we give you a specific reference but a quick look at a contents page or in an index will find you what you want.

We think you'll find the following books useful on this subject (the first two are referred to throughout the text):

D.A. Buchanan and A.A. Huczynski, *Organisational Behaviour*, Prentice Hall, London, 1985.

C.B. Handy, *Understanding Organisations*, Penguin, London, 1986.

This one is an excellent textbook with good illustrations and an admirable breadth of cover and economy of text:

G.J. Cohen, *The Nature of Management*, Graham & Trotman, London, 1985.

Invaluable practice and advice on answering the ubiquitous case-study type of question are given in:

Bill Braddick, *Nature of Management Case Studies*, The Institute of Bankers, London, 1985.

The post-tests

The final section consists of 10 *post-tests*. These also use MCQs but this time you're just told which answer is correct.

You'll find that the post-tests largely retest what was covered in the main MCQs. This is deliberate. The purpose of the post-tests is to assess the progress you've made in your revision campaign.

You may wish to answer them all together — a kind of mock exam if you like — and record your scores — *two* marks for each correct answer — on the Score Grid. You can then compare your score with those on the corresponding Short Answer Test and Main MCQ Test. While the comparisons won't be 'scientific', you will get a good indication of the effectiveness of your revision.

What do I do when I've finished?

If you work through this book properly and revise conscientiously following our guidance, you should be well prepared for the exam. However, if the post-tests reveal that you still have some areas of weakness you'll have to go back and revise these again — at least you'll know which ones they are and how to go about it!

Finally, remember our general advice on exam technique. The best of luck; we're sure you'll do well.

David Palfreman *Editor*
Brian Stone *Author*

Short Answer Tests

Start your revision by attempting the short answer tests on pages 2 to 6. There are 6 marks for each question.

Questions

Topic 1 Organizations

1 What are
   line management?
   staff management?
2 Briefly describe the three main ideal types of organization,
   according to Max Weber.
3 What is meant, in classical organization theory, by
   a the scalar chain?
   b the parity principle?
   c unity of command?
4 What were the main findings of Elton Mayo's reports on the
   Hawthorne Experiments?
5 What is meant by the term 'contingency theory'?
6 What two principal forms of organization are described by Burns
   and Stalker? What are their main characteristics?
7 Explain how the technology of production affects organizational
   structure.
8 Draw a diagram of a simple open system.
9 In a modern organization, what are
   a differentiation?
   b integration?
10 What are the main characteristics of a bureaucratic type of
    organization?

Answers on page 7

Topic 2 The banking environment

1 Name three demographic factors which influence people's attitudes
   towards their colleagues, as co-workers or as neighbours.
2 What proportion of your bank's staff at Grade 4 are female? What
   proportion at Grade 1?
3 Name at least three ways in which people can borrow money other
   than from clearing banks, HP or building societies.
4 Why do banks from time to time offer 'free banking if in credit', an
   expensive business for them?
5 Name one service offered by a bank other than your own, and
   briefly describe its operation and benefits.

6   Write three *brief* statements about the standard policies of each of the Conservative, the Labour and the SDP/Liberal Alliance parties.

7   What do you think is the single most noticeable technological change in banking that the customer will have noticed in the last five years?

8   And which change is most noticeable to bank staff?

9   Name three technological changes you realistically expect in the next five years, which will alter banking as it is now.

10   What would you personally receive in redundancy payments under your bank's scheme if you were to be given notice today?

Answers on page 9

Topic 3   Managerial roles and processes

1   What is a role?

2   How do people handle role conflict?

3   Name two of the informational roles as described by Henry Mintzberg.

4   What kind of character does a 'shaper' have, according to Belbin?

5   Of the various stages in the managerial process, which relate specifically to the future?

6   And which relate specifically to getting things done presently, marshalling resources and allocating tasks?

7   Give examples of role requirements as they relate to the role of 'life and soul of the party'.

8   What does the branch manager have to do as 'figurehead'? Illustrate your answer with examples.

9   What is the major difference between the 'resource allocator' and the 'plant'?

10   Give a hypothetical example of a manager visibly exercising the control function of the managerial process.

Answers on page 11

Topic 4   Managerial techniques and tools

1   How do you segment a market?

2   What is the difference between field research and desk research?

1   On a questionnaire, what is the difference between an open and a closed question?

4   What do you do in the criteria stage of decision making?

3

5   What is the formula for calculating the optimum course of action when making a decision?
6   In both decision making and problem solving, what are the actions which need to be taken after the intellectual/data stages have been completed?
7   What is the difference between planning and forecasting?
8   What is recorded as a budgeted set of actions unfold?
9   What is the critical path?
10 How is the manager's agreement normally obtained to the objectives set in a 'management by objectives' scheme?

Answers on page 13

Topic 5   Communication

1   Give three examples of formal communication situations at work.
2   What is a semantic barrier to communication? Give at least one example.
3   What is a psychological barrier to communication? Give at least one example.
4   In terms of the traditional model of communication, explain why jargon is a problem in communication.
5   What are the main benefits and drawbacks to the use of visual posters on the office noticeboard for conveying information to the staff?
6   What is the name of your house-journal? What are its overall objectives? Name the house-journal of at least one other bank.
7   Give a definition of an 'interview'.
8   What is the difference between 'counselling' and 'giving advice'?
9   What must managers do to prepare themselves for a briefing before delivering it to staff?
10 Give three examples of recent innovations in office technology concerned with communication, and explain their basic functions.

Answers on page 15

Topic 6   Leadership and management style

1   Who was responsible for the concept of situational leadership, and what was the definition of this?
2   What are the three sets of group needs suggested in action-centred leadership?
3   Why is 9,9 management more effective than 1,1?

4 What are the four points on the management style continuum as outlined by Tannenbaum and Schmidt?
5 State any two traits or qualities you believe a leader should have.
6 Why is the idea of 'leadership qualities' not believed to be as useful as it used to be?
7 What are the three dimensions in Reddin's 3D model?
8 What are the two main kinds of leader described in Fiedler's theory of leadership effectiveness?
9 What is the difference between a formal and an informal leader?
10 How could a leader motivate the individual, according to Adair?

Answers on page 17

Topic 7 Motivation

1 Give a working definition of human need.
2 What are hygiene factors? Define and give examples.
3 What does 'self actualization' mean?
4 When does a set of human needs become 'prepotent'?
5 What is 'valency'? Why does it matter to a manager who wants to motivate staff?
6 What is 'theory X'?
7 What is the difference between satisfiers and dissatisfiers?
8 'I'm a Grade 2': what is technically wrong with this statement?
9 Give three examples of constituents of a rewards package.
10 Why are 'ego needs' so important in motivating bank staff?

Answers on page 19

Topic 8 Personnel practices

1 What does manpower planning have in common with basic economics?
2 Name some of the elements affecting the organization's demand for manpower.
3 What is the result to the organization of the ideal perfect job advertisement?
4 Name four of the points of the NIIP seven point plan.
5 What is meant by 'two-tier' recruitment?
6 How can you evaluate the effectiveness of training?
7 Who or what benefits from effective training?
8 Name some of the methods of off-the-job training.
9 What are the problems caused by appraisals being annual?

10 What scales are used by your bank's appraisal scheme?

Answers on page 21

Topic 9   Groups

1 Whose research in the 1920s concluded that work is a group activity?
2 What is the difference between a formal and an informal group?
3 What are primary and secondary groups?
4 What is it that distinguishes a work group from a family group?
5 What did Tuckman say were the four stages in the development of a group?
6 Why is a group boundary so called?
7 What are the advantages and disadvantages of group decision making?
8 For what reasons do people conform to group norms?
9 What can groups do about people who do not conform?
10 What group needs do good leaders satisfy?

Answers on page 22

Topic 10   Industrial relations

1 What is collective bargaining?
2 What is the name of the body which represents the employers in negotiations between the banks and their staff?
3 What is the Clearing Banks' general attitude towards staff's union membership, and why?
4 What was BIFU called before it changed its name? When and why did it do so?
5 On what principal topics do the Clearing Banks and the Unions negotiate? Name at least three such topics.
6 What was the main item of concern of the Bullock enquiry?
7 What is a grievance procedure? What is the first step to be taken in involving your bank's grievance procedure?
8 Suggest three chracteristics which define an interaction between one party and another as 'negotiation'.
9 What was Dr Tom Johnston's project concerned with in relation to collective bargaining in the banking industry?
10 When was the last successful nationwide strike in the banking industry? What was it about, and what was the result?

Answers on page 24

Answers

Topic 1   Organizations

1   Line management has direct responsibilities for the work and objectives of the organization, converting input into output (1 mark). Responsibility (and authority and communication) is conventionally vertical, from senior management to junior operatives (e.g. branch management, chief cashier). Staff management is advisory and consultant. It comprises specialists or experts working across the 'lines' of line management, providing a service and resources to support them in furthering the company objectives (e.g. personnel department, computer services. (1 mark).

/1

/1

2   *Charismatic*, following extraordinary individuals with exceptional characteristics (Genghis Khan, for example); *traditional*, following leaders who have inherited their position by well-established, laid-down rules from the past; *rational/legal* or *bureaucratic*: impersonal, hierarchic, specialized and qualified staff, central records (see question 10) (2 marks for all three; 1 mark for any two).

/2

3   **a** Clear lines of defined authority from top to bottom.
b Responsibility should equal authority; or, whatever one is supposed to do, one is given the power to do.
c Everyone should have one boss, and know who it is. (2 marks for all three; 1 mark for any two.)

/2

4   Work is a *group* activity, not individual or mass; people like to feel *special* and consulted about their work; there are *informal* groups in organizations as well as formal, and these can powerfully determine output; *human relationships* between people and their bosses, as well as with each other, are important to the work (2 marks for all three; 1 mark for any one).

/2

5   The structure, practices and philosophy of an organization depend on its internal and external

7

circumstances, and should be adjusted accordingly. /2

6 Organismic: like an organism; changing rapidly and flexibly to cope with a volatile environment (1 mark). /1
Mechanistic: like a machine; inflexible, rule-controlled, working according to custom and practice in stable environments (1 mark). /1

7 If the name Joan Woodward isn't in your answer, no marks! She says that organization structures vary from very shallow to many layers of authority as technology ranges from one-off through batch production, mass production and continuous flow (from your personal tailor through to Shell). /2

8 You should have included at least the following for 2 marks:

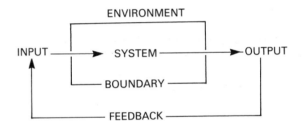

/2

9 a Varying the nature, structure and management style of environment-facing sections of the organization according to the changeability of the environment (1 mark). /1
b Having methods to coordinate and control differentiated sections of the organization so that it functions effectively overall, via 'linking pin' mechanisms (1 mark). /1

10 No excuses for placing this question 'out of sequence'. You must know the Weberian (and after) concept of bureaucracy, and have *rational*, *rehearsed* and *planned* ways of applying it to your bank or division or department — no ranting and raving: it irritates examiners. Briefly:

Continuity: business as usual, regardless of personalities and their presence or absence.

Your score

Qualification: positions divided into functions, specialized, and filled with those best qualified for them.

Specification: of job-content, of rules of limits of responsibility and discipline, of authority.

Hierarchy: clear top-to-bottom lines of authority and communication, of who reports to/talks to whom.

Written records (the 'bureau'): no transaction but that it is centrally recorded, with rules of access. (2 marks for four; 1 mark for two.)

/2

➡ *your total score for this Topic* . . . . /20

Topic 2   The banking environment

1   Give yourself two marks for any three (always answer the question, in this sense) of race, sex, age, social class, occupation, organizational status, income, educational standard, geographical origin: if you gave these or other such answers, it shows you know what 'demographic' means!

/2

2   Well, we can't answer this — but your Personnel Department can — or if you don't work for a clearing bank, the Institute of Bankers, BIFU or the Banking Information Service can. Do find out: it's the kind of statistic examiners like (if appropriate to the question, and accurate. . . . . .) (2 marks if you are within 10% — when you find out the answer!)

/2

3   Again, any three from Access, Barclaycard, charge cards like Diners' Club, American Express, store cards, finance companies, insurance companies, home catalogue companies, their relatives and friends, their employers, suppliers, and probably others: a reflection on the true competitive environment. (2 marks for three, 1 for one or two.)

/2

4   Because they are in a *fiercely competitive market* in which the *customer's sophistication is increasing*. Loyalty is no longer paramount: in 1985 nearly half a million accounts switched to one clearing bank offering free

9

banking. (Award yourselves 2 marks if you concen-
trated on competition.)

/2

5 Once again, we cannot answer that. But you can find
out by strolling into a competitor's branch, and
taking their leaflets. Please do this: a major part of
your bank's environment is the other banks, and it
will give you a competitive examination edge to use
examples from more than one bank. The examiner is
looking for economic awareness in future banking
managers. (Two marks for describing a service you
know is offered by another bank.)

/2

6 *Conservatives*
   Encourage free enterprise
   Believe in free market forces
   Are in favour of private medicine/education
   Seek to curtail public spending
   Seek to reduce direction taxation
   Promote property/house ownership
   Strongly support military deterrence
   Supports and is supported by large businesses

The Labour Party
   Believes in public ownership of certain 'national
      assets' like railways
   Promotes a strong Welfare State
   Is not in favour of private education/medicine
   Supports and is supported by the Trades Unions
   Believes in progressive taxation
   Promotes the development of council housing
   Believes in military disarmament
   Seeks overall economic equality, but does not
      deny differential on seniority or merit.

The SDP/Liberal Alliance
   Believes in proportional representation
   Is in favour of government share ownership
   Adopts ad-hoc problem solving rather than set
      policies on all issues
   Seeks reform of the rates system, to tax the value
      of land
   Is in favour of minimal military deterrence
   Believes in equal educational opportunity
   Is supported by (high) membership subscription
(Difficult to get 2 marks on this one — but 2 if you

answered in full, and 1 if you could make ONE   /2
statement about each party.)

7   To answer this, put yourself in their shoes (stand
    outside your bank, or bandit screen). You could have
    said cash dispensers, and you probably did —
    because most of the other technological changes are
    not noticeable by your cutomers, except perhaps the
    form of their statements. (2 for cash dispensers; 2
    for statements; allow yourself a sensible 1 mark for   /2
    other technology.)

8   You tell me: but I suspect that the cash dispenser
    must also come into this, or changes in computer
    operations, or video communication systems, or
    document transmission systems, or word processing,
    or the manager's micro (or, far more probably, the
    customer's micro) (2 for any of these.)   /2

9   Electronic fund transfer at point of sale (EFTPoS);
    new cash dispenser services, e.g. paying bills; 'home
    banking' via microcomputer/Prestel; building society
    link-ups and 'clearing'; intelligent cards, or debit
    cards (like Cardphone); interactive video system,
    internal and customer-facing; others you know of.
    (2 marks for three; 1 for one or two of these.)   /2

10 And finally, we can't answer that either: but you can,
    and you should find out. Reflect how you might
    survive, and actually formulate in a series of short
    statements your *considered* thoughts on the current
    situation concerning the national employment
    situation. Using the exact figure you've obtained
    from the Personnel Department, or the appropriate
    manual, by the way, *will* impress the examiner, if
    appropriate and accurate. (2 marks for a confident
    figure in your mind; or for knowing — and be honest
    — exactly how you can find out.)   /2

your total score for this Topic . . . . /20

Topic 3   Managerial roles and processes

1   A role is a set of norms, expectations, rules of
    behaviour and dress and speech, which fits into a set

of other roles: 2 marks for something close to this. It usually has a label or title or name, like 'Managing Director', 'Bank Clerk', 'Mother Hen' or 'Office Comedian', and anyone filling the role is expected to behave in the same general way as anyone else in such a role.

/2

2   In a few different but expectable ways. Role conflict is difficulty in choosing between two appropriate roles, like a Tutor having to reprimand a student who is also a Friend: as tutor the reprimand may be essential; as friend the relationship could be damaged. Three ways to handle this could be: to opt out, and have someone else solve the problem; or to compartmentalize, and determine to choose and behave firmly in one (and therefore *not* the other); or to appeal for advice, help and support to a higher authority in the choice of action. A mark for suggesting one of these, and one for thinking of an example.

/2

3   2 marks for *two* from Figurehead, Leader, Liaison.

/2

4   The Shaper is a strong role, dominant and driving, pressing the group to try new activities, full of nervous/emotional energy.

/2

5   *Setting objectives*: to set up the targets for which the group must aim in the short, medium and long term. *Forecasting*: to gather information and extrapolate trends to form a picture of the probable course of events. *Planning*: setting forth sets of actions to achieve the objectives set in the light of the forecasts. (2 marks for all three; 1 mark for two.)

/2

6   Organization/coordination: seeing to it that all the current resources are being efficiently used, not without regard to the planned future actions and the group's ongoing needs.

/2

7   Role requirements are the specifications for anyone filling the role from those who impinge on it. 2 marks for any three, 1 for any two of the following:

To be cheerful on all occasions at the party
To provide amusement to partygoers
To suggest diverting activities at the party

To originate and take responsibility for practical jokes

Your score

To cheer up any who are not in the party spirit.

/2

8   The manager must represent the organization on formal occasions (1 mark). Examples might be attendance at the Institute Dinner, chair the Institute annual quiz, speak at the local Rotary Club, present School Prizes, and so on (a mark for any two, or any two similar).

/2

9   The Resource Allocator is relaxed, outgoing, public-relations oriented, host and socialiser (1 mark); the Plant is inward-thinking, reflective, introspective, intellectual and idea-providing (1 mark).

/2

10 Many: but for example doing a tour of the office to see that plans are being carried out; having inter-mittent planned, or regular meetings to review progress; seeing to it that charts recording steps towards an objective are kept up to date; calling for information obviously to assess the current state of a project, and so on (1 mark each for any two: but they must have been *visible* in answer to the question).

/2

your total score for this Topic . . . . /20

Topic 4   Managerial techniques and tools

1   A market is segmented when a careful analytical section is defined by the marketer (2 marks for an answer similar to this). For instance, a maker of high-class religious articles based in Manchester might not choose to see the entire general public as his market, but only those who are of the appropriate religion, who are religious enough to buy the articles and of a sufficiently high income to afford them, and living close to his retail outlet. The marketer could then determine where the advertising should be placed, what transport and distribution were needed, the size and financial extent of his market, which specific religious leaders to cultivate, and other data to make sales and income forecasts.

/2

13

2   Field research is done out where the data needs to be collected and in direct contact with the sources of that data, such as by questionnaire in a shopping centre (1 mark); desk research is done at home, in libraries or other sources of recorded data (1 mark). /2

3   A closed question gives predeterminable ranges of answers so that boxes can be ticked by the questioner (1 mark); an open question permits the answerer to give unstructured responses according to choice (usually beginning with 'what', 'how' or 'why') (1 mark). /1 /1

4   In the Criteria stage you set criteria against which you will compare alternative courses of action; those which exceed the criteria will be considered for choice. /2

5   Multiply the utility — the value of the action — by its probability, the chances of its happening. /2

6   The action must be *implemented* and the first steps taken to ensure that it is under way; it must be *communicated* so that all involved are aware of what is happening; and it must be *monitored* so that any adjustments which need to be made for its success are in fact made. Give yourself 1 mark for any one; 2 for any two. /2

7   Planning is setting *courses of action* to deal with future environments and events (1 mark). Forecasting is *making predictions* about those environments (1 mark). The past and present give the basis for the forecast, and the forecast does the same for the plans. /2

8   The *expected* events or results or figures; the *actual* ones; and the *variance*, being the difference in actual or proportional terms between the expected and the actual (2 marks for all three; 1 for any two). /2

9   It is the longest inevitable series of events in a project, shorter than which the project cannot be, and around which, when it is calculated, all the other project plans are adjusted. /2

10   By the boss involving the manager from the beginning, so that by open, full and detailed

discussion, agreement is reached about the stringency and attainability of all targets in the manager's key areas. (The manager's agreement is also encouraged, by the way, by setting reward levels commensurate with the importance of the achievement of the objectives to the organization.)

Your score

/2

➤*your total score for this Topic* . . . . /20

Topic 5   Communication

1   You could have said interviewing for discipline or grievance; counselling; briefing; appraisal; meetings and conferences; operating the terminal; circulars; training courses and sessions; or any situation in which one person or body communicates with another to convey information. Give yourself 1 mark for identifying one; 2 marks for three.

/2

2   A semantic barrier to communication is a barrier formed by the ineffective use of language or symbols — 1 mark for an answer close to this definition. Another mark for an appropriate example, such as talking French to an Albanian, or referring to the in-clearing to most members of the public, or writing this book in Arabic script for most of its readers.

/2

3   A psychological barrier is one formed by the psychology of either the persons sending the message or the intended recipient, something in their make-up preventing them from sending or receiving the message efficiently. 1 mark for a definition close to this. Another for an example such as not sending poor performance figures to the boss because you're afraid of his reaction; or the boss not believing those figures because you are both modest and beautiful in the boss's eyes. . . . .

/2

4   In terms of the traditional model, jargon is an encoded communication language which is not a problem, in fact, if correctly decoded, but becomes one when the destination's decoder fails to translate it correctly (2 marks *only* if you used the words 'code'

or 'encoded'). Note, please, that it is *data* which is transmitted; it only becomes *information* when translated — decoded — and understood.

5 Visual information is immediate; attractive; memorable; has impact; can be dramatic. It can, however, convey information which is limited; no elaboration is possible; it can be stilted (corny!); it becomes stale quickly; it needs special skills; notices are sometimes 'censored', or not left visible for long enough (2 marks for two advantages and two disadvantages).

/2

6 *You* answer the first part! Its objectives can vary, but they tend to be motivational and integrative, giving a feeling of belonging to the corporate body; to keep staff (*and* pensioners and certain customers) in touch with staff movements and developments; to be informative about company changes and developments; and to act as an internal and external organ of public relations. (A mark for the name of your own *and* one other; a mark for two distinct objectives). Try and get to see the house-journal of another bank. It will give you a new perspective on communication in their and your own bank (they do not tend to be confidential), and to be able to name more than one will impress the examiners with your wide interest in banking!

/2

7 Something like 'a formal interaction between (at least) two people with stated objectives, planned and structured, employing investigatory techniques to come to decisional conclusions in the course of day-to-day activities'; check whether yours contained most of these elements, and give yourself 2 marks if it did.

/2

8 'Giving advice' means just that; but basically a counselling session extracts and supports courses of action decided upon by the person counselled: advice is usually only given on the request of or by the consent of the person counselled (2 marks).

/2

9 Clearly understand the task to be briefed; prepare the briefing itself, including the logistics, 'stage management', own verbal section; prepare the materials to be issued as part of the briefing. (2 marks for all of these; 1 for one or two of them.)

/2

10 The examiners will expect the newly qualified Associate to be aware of current technological developments, *and* on the whole to be favourably inclined towards them as efficient tools of tomorrow's management. You could have cited wordprocessors, microcomputers with database or spreadsheet packages, conference-devices on telephones, teletext facilities on television sets, videotape recorders; and you would have to have explained their use. (2 marks for each device/explanation.)

Your score /2

your total score for this Topic .... /20

Topic 6   Leadership and management style

1 Mary Parker Follett (1 mark); and that different situations called for different leaders, so that within a group one person could be leader when the task was in his/her sphere of expertise, handing over leadership to another when the task changed in nature (1 mark).

/1

/1

2 The *task* needs, to get the job done, to be rid of backlog, to perform well intrinsically and in comparison with other similar groups; the *team* needs, sometimes called morale or group maintenance needs, to keep the group together, keep spirits high, maintain discipline, trust and cohesion; and *individual* needs, for personal satisfaction, achieved recognition in the work situation (2 marks only for all three).

/2

3 These numbers refer to Blake and Mouton's Managerial Grid (Blake's Grid, for short). 1,1 is the bottom left hand corner of a two-dimensional graph, with 1 (low) for Concern-for-People, and 1 for Concern-for-Production. 9,9 is the top right-hand corner, with the top mark for Concern for both People and Production (2 marks if you know all this).

/2

4 *Autocratic* in which the manager takes all decisions and delivers them as orders; *benevolent autocratic*, in which the orders are presented as for the good of the staff, as is punishment for non-compliance; *consult-*

ative, where the manager asks staff for opinions and takes them into account before making decisions; and *participative,* in which the group make the decisions and the manager marshalls resources to implement them. (2 marks for all four; 1 for any three correct.)

/2

5   There are many you could state, and these will be as a result of your reading or experience. Be prepared to defend them critically and logically, with examples of their usefulness; and give yourself 2 marks if you can honestly say you can. Note also the answer to the next question.

/2

6   Because a comprehensive list of such qualities would be impossibly long; because the list would not be agreed by any two experts; because different experts would define each trait-word slightly differently; because different traits would be appropriate in different leadership situations; because items on the list might not apply to obviously great leaders; and because people possessing most of the qualities might still not be good leaders (among other reasons. . . . . . .). (2 marks for any two, 1 for one.)

/2

7   Task Orientation (TO); Relationship Orientation (RO); Effectiveness (E). (2 marks for all three; 1 for any two.)

/2

8   The task oriented leader, who is principally concerned for the output of the organization, and who functions best when certain work and staff conditions are, oddly enough, either very favourable *or* very unfavourable; and the relationship oriented manager, concerned for harmony, who is more effective when conditions are neither favourable nor unfavourable. A mark for each.

/2

9   The formal leader is the one appointed by or recognized by the management of the organization (1 mark), while the informal leader is appointed by or recognized by the group led (1 mark). It could be the same person (cf. Topic 9, Groups).

/2

10   By satisfying that individual's needs in the group (2 marks for this or a close answer), thus enabling him/her to contribute to getting the task done and

improving morale. Reference might be made here to Maslow's Hierarchy of Needs — next topic — and how each level can be satisfied at work by action centred leadership; now read on........

Your score

/2

━━━▷ *your total score for this Topic* .... /20

Topic 7   Motivation

1   You could answer this in a number of ways, but it's probably referring to Maslow, and his definition would be something like 'the difference between the state you are actually in and the state you'd like to be in'. Motivation is the drive to reduce that difference (2 marks for this or a close answer).

/2

2   Hygiene factors — Herzberg's concept — are those factors at work which, *if absent*, cause dissatisfaction (see Answer 7 below) (1 mark). Examples would be the quality of work conditions, relationships with supervisors, the company's bureaucratic restrictions, basic pay, relationships with colleagues (1 mark for any of these).

/1

/1

3   Self actualization is Maslow's term for the height of human motivation: when all else is satisfied, people want to fulfil the potential which they know to exist in them (2 marks, especially if you used the word 'fulfil' or 'fulfilment').

/2

4   Maslow again — but his theory is central, and these key words show examiners that you have studied — and a need becomes 'prepotent' when a lower order of need is satisfied: if I am no longer hungry because I have eaten, my safety needs will become prepotent and I will seek the means to secure my lines to the next series of meals (2 marks).

/2

5   Valency is a short term for the perceived value of a reward to the person receiving it (1 mark). Nobody will be motivated to work for anything which is of no value; and the utility in a reward depends more importantly on the receiver's perception than that of the donor (1 mark). It is a term normally used in

'expectancy theory', which postulates a simple equation combining valency with expectancy, the perceived probability that the performance will lead to reward: Level of Motivation = Expectancy × Valency.

/2

6 McGregor said that at the extremes of managerial attitudes were two theories, X and Y: theory X is the view that unless you do something to workers they will not work. They have no natural drive, creativity or desire for responsibility and achievement (2 marks).

/2

7 Satisfiers are factors at work which, if present or good, give positive feelings of satisfaction (1 mark). Dissatisfiers, if absent or bad, give positive feelings of dissatisfaction (1 mark). The distinction is like the difference between pleasure and pain: giving pleasure is a different process from removing pain (which can be simultaneously and independently needed).

/2

8 In the clearing bank's grading system, as in most others, it is the job which is graded, not the incumbent. You are not a Grade 2: you are a clerk occupying a Grade 2 post (2 marks).

/2

9 Salary, pensions, paid holidays, cheap loans, car schemes, bonuses, productivity incentives, preferential mortgages, free product, medical insurance, other fringe benefits (2 marks if you could name three — no marks if you couldn't).

/2

10 Ego needs are the needs for recognition as an individual, the need to feel special or expert or acceptable as a contributing group member. Tangibly, a banker can have this need satisfied by promotion; or less tangibly, by being given specific responsibility in a field of expertise, major or minor. To make it effective as a motivating factor, management would have to ensure that the given responsibility is seen by the receiver as distinguishing that person as special (2 marks).

/2

 *your total score for this Topic* . . . . /20

Topic 8   Personnel practices

1   Supply and demand as a central concept (2 marks): manpower planning has to do with forecasting and planning for changes in the supply and the demand in the organization of the right people in the right jobs at the right time.

/2

2   You could have named anything which will alter in the future to call for more or less staff in one or another area of the bank, such as a planned merger or takeover, radical differences in the lifestyles of the customers, technological developments, foreseen patterns of retirement and so on (1 mark for any two; 2 for any three).

/2

3   One single application for the job, from the single perfect candidate: think about it! (and give yourself 2 marks. . . . .).

/2

4   2 marks for any four from: physical make-up, attainments, general intelligence, special aptitudes, interests, disposition, and circumstances. (2 marks for any three).

/2

5   Recruiting certain people with an eye to long-term career development (1 mark), and certain others to fill specific jobs who are not expected to progress (1 mark). This contrasts with what atually happens in banks, which is multi-tier recruitment with a variety of plans for future work prospects.

/2

6   Principally by making clear statements, *before* the training, of the training objectives (1 mark), and by *measuring* the candidate's ability in the area being trained before and after the training in terms of the objectives (1 mark).

/2

7   The *organization* by having a more appropriately skilled workforce; the local *management* by having a flexible, competent and motivated staff; the *candidate* by having pride and confidence in new abilities (2 marks for these or sensible answers — not 'don't know').

/2

8   Internal courses; external courses; short/medium/ long term secondments, in-bank or external; video

programmes; programmed learning texts; Institute of Bankers studies; books (2 marks for any three of these, none for less.)

9   2 for any two, and 1 for any one, from:

Difficulty in remembering early incidents or achievements; rare incentive for reluctant manager to assess staff abilities; difficulty in formal monitoring of last year's suggested actions; possibility of occurrence every year at low/bad/poor-performance occasion; other reasons you may have thought of! (Remember that while you are expected to be systematic, you are also given credit for common sense — or at least high-calibre common sense. . . . .)

 /2

10   Only you and your own-bank colleagues can answer that; but be it 1 to 6 or A to E, or 0 to 100%, you should know about it to use as illustration in the exam, and even better if you know of the scheme of at least one other bank. 2 marks if you do know — but an unmarked pat on the back if you know of another bank's scales!

 /2

 *your total score for this Topic* . . . . /20

Topic 9   Groups

1   Elton Mayo and his team (1 mark), during the Hawthorne Experiments (1 mark), observed that some of their subjects' behaviour could be attributed to group membership: where they felt they belonged, and were regarded as special either by group members or their management, their willingness to work towards group levels of productivity — and not necessarily company levels — was heightened. /2

2   A formal group is one set up or recognized by the work organization in which it is set, and has tasks, aims, roles and structure which are more or less specific (1 mark). An informal group is created by its members who may have a mutual interest or characteristic (1 mark). /2

22

3   The primary group is one which regularly interacts on a day-to-day basis, with usually between four and twelve members (1 mark). The secondary group is one in which the members have something in common, and meet less frequently and possibly only on formal occasions, such as an association of the Chief Executives of the clearing banks (1 mark).

/2

4   A work group has tasks and objectives, which are its reason for existing. 2 marks if this was the specific point you made. Interestingly, the aims of *informal* groups which have the same members as the formal group tend to take precedence. This is particularly true when formal aims, objectives or targets are unclear or not well communicated.

/2

5   2 marks for getting all these right *and* in the right order: 1 for three, or four in the wrong order:

Forming, when they come together and set up methods of operation; *storming*, when they have conflict in adjusting those methods; *norming*, when they settle those conflicts and have workable rules; and *performing*, when they begin to achieve positive results.

/2

6   2 marks for saying that it's because it is a clear 'line' around a group defining who is inside, who is out, and having clear rules about access, either temporary or permanent.

/2

7   Group decisions have the advantage of pooling the resources of experience, knowledge and ability of the group. They are usually agreed by the group when made, and commit all members to working to implement them — 1 mark for any of these. However, they are time consuming to make, all members must be present when they are made, they are difficult to change, and they cause internal problems where there is one or more dissenter (1 more mark for any of these).

/2

8   Partly because they are inclined to, where they have joined the group voluntarily — they wanted to be in that group with those norms; partly because it signifies their acceptance of the group and then the group's acceptance of them, satisfying their affilia-

tion or social needs; and partly because groups have sanctions, ways of putting pressure in deviants, from disapproval through to downright dismissal (2 marks for any of these).

/2

9   They can show disapproval non-verbally (by looks and deeds); by actively telling off ('we don't do *that* sort of thing in this section'); by removing privileges ('unless you agree, you're not having lunch with us'); by suspending communication altogether ('sending to Coventry'); by expulsion from the informal group ('you're just not one of *us* any more'); by pressure to expulsion from the formal group ('unless *she* goes, none of us is continuing to work'). 1 mark for one, 2 for two of these.

/2

10 They satisfy the *task* needs, to get jobs done by, for example, setting targets, obtaining resources; the *team* needs for morale, by praising where appropriate and by resolving conflict; and *individual* needs, e.g. by encouraging the staff and giving them work to do that they like or are good at. (2 marks for all three, 1 for any two of these.)

/2

your total score for this Topic . . . . /20

Topic 10   Industrial relations

1   Collective bargaining is a process in which (at least) two parties, usually representing employers on the one hand and employees on the other, attempt to reach agreement on wages or conditions of work (1 mark) via agreed procedures (1 mark).

/2

2   The Federation of London Clearing Banks Employers, or FLCBE — in England and Wales, that is; if you live elsewhere, find out what the name of the local body is, and be able to quote it accurately (2 marks).

/2

3   They encourage it (2 marks) not merely permit it (1 mark), and positively offer facilities for staff to engage in union activities. This is because the more

Your score

people are members, the more likely it is that the unions with whom they negotiate represent a majority; and the more likely there is to be a number of moderate members rather than just union enthusiasts; and the more effective negotiation is.

/2

4 National Union of Bank Employees (1 mark); 1979, to represent staff in Insurance and Finance and other related industries (1 mark).

/2

5 2 marks for any three from:

— salaries Grades 1 to 4
— minimum managerial salary, first appointment
— safety at work
— working hours
— holidays, clerical (unappointed) staff
— large town, London and other territorial allowances.

/2

6 Industrial democracy: the right of workers to a say in organizational decisions affecting their working lives (2 marks).

/2

7 A grievance procedure is a formal route, agreed by staff and employer's representatives, whereby a hearing can be given, and redress obtained, in the case of an employee having a genuine complaint about treatment at work (1 mark). The first step depends on your bank's procedure: information about the procedure ought to be freely available to you, so you get your other mark if you know the answer to part 2 of the question!

/2

8 Many: 2 marks for any three: three very clear ones are:

— (at least) two parties starting from conflicting positions
— a genuine desire for eventual agreement
— a measure of power residing in each party.

/2

9 The issue of representation; the conflict between the Clearing Banks Union, formerly the Confederation of Bank Staff Associations (CBSA), and BIFU; the possibility of merger and the formation of a single clearing banks union. It was not successful (2 marks for any two of the above).

/2

10   In 1967 (1 mark). It was intended to force the
     employing banks to recognize and grant representa-
     tion and negotiating rights to the trade union, then
     the National Union of Bank Employees, NUBE
     (1 mark). It was successful, and machinery was set
     up for national negotiation on a series of issues in
     the following year.

Your score

/2

➡ *your total score for this Topic* . . . . /20

When you have completed all the short answer tests, fill in your
score on the score grid (inside the back cover). You can now use
your results in this section to rank your revision priorities,
starting with your weakest topic first.

Topics

For each topic, start with the study guide and then try to answer the multiple choice questions which follow.

Topic 1   Organizations

Study guide

This is the part of the syllabus least directly related to the practice of management, but the examiner will expect you to have an *accurate* knowledge of the people who have written about the theory of organization and what they said. Unfortunately, textbooks tend to differ about exactly who said what among early theorists, so if you're confused, it's not just you. . . . Here you will find a summary of what most writers agree on.

In general overview, organization theory can be divided for the sake of revision into six: Weber/Bureaucracy, Classical Theory, Human Relations, Systems Thinking, Contingency Theory, Design ('OD').

Weber

Max Weber wrote (in German) in the late nineteenth/early twentieth century. He was interested in authority structures, and what legitimizes them — why the members permit the bosses to exercise authority over them. He characterized three main types of organized authority structure:

Charismatic
Those follow the leader who has an element in his/her personality which makes that leader special, extraordinary, even superhuman, such people as Alexander, Julius Caesar, the Duke of Wellington; or Henry Ford, Lord Sieff of Marks & Spencer, Michael Edwardes. Such organizations benefit during the leader's lifetime, but unless there is a highly unlikely coincidence, a charismatic successor is hard to find and the organizational authority type will probably change to one of the other two.

Traditional
Those in charge have power because there is a laid-down precedent: they have inherited the position, or they are in some other way the *clearly specified successor*. People in specific positions have the power that people in those positions have always had, and custom and practice are the watchwords. Examples are hereditary posts (the Earl Marshall's office), old family firms, and possibly more recent ones — the Ewings of Dallas have a number of traditional-type elements in their organization!

Rational/legal, or bureaucratic

'Bureau-cratic' actually means 'Rule of the Office' — Office Rules OK — which will remind you of the essence of bureaucracy: it's not the person but the office held to which the authority belongs. Some characteristics:

— Continuity: business as usual, regardless of presence/absence of persons involved
— Qualification: posts held by those trained and qualified
— Office-based rules: job specifications indicate responsibility, authority, discipline power
— Hierarchy: authority and power from the top to the bottom along clear unambiguous routes
— The 'bureau': written records of all activity with rules of access, held centrally.

Organizational Behaviour, p. 318:– Buchanan and Huczynski: Prentice Hall.

Classical organization theory

Unless you wish to take your study further, you don't really need to know what Taylor said that Urwick didn't, or the distinction between Fayol and Follett. Do read at least one good textbook about these writers, and then *carefully* learn the central elements of 'classical theory' — headings below, but see that you can expand on these and that you know what the jargon words actually mean, like 'scalar' and 'parity' etc.

— Continuity: The organization, posts, structure do not depend on the person filling them, but have a separate specified existence.

— Specialization: Jobs are divided into sub-elements and people are specially selected and trained to do their own small part of them.

— Scalar principle: Authority goes in straight lines from above to below in a clear hierarchy.

— Parity principle: Authority in a post should equal its responsibility: one should have the given power to carry out one's due tasks.

— Unity of command: Each subordinate should have to report to only one boss.

— Unity of direction: All the elements in an organization should be directed to one (set of) objective(s).

— Corporate interest: Individual interests will always be subordinate to the corporate interests.

— Span of control: No boss will have more than five or six subordinates.

— Coordination: The elements of an organization will be coordinated, deliberately, by people in coordinating positions.

You will find this list in your textbooks, but look out for different terminology — after all, Henri Fayol, one of the early listers of such principles, wrote in French!

 Organizational Behaviour, p. 338: Buchanan and Huczynski: Prentice Hall.

Human relations

'Human relations' does not mean the manager being Mr or Mrs Nice Guy. It is a school of management thought which insists that good management clearly understands people and the relationships between them, using this understanding to advance corporate objectives.

You *must* know what the Hawthorne Experiments were, and what the central conclusions were. A good textbook will give you the full rundown — please read, absorb and note — but essentially there were two main sets of experiment:

The relay assembly test room, in which it was observed that whatever was done to alter the working, pay and work/leisure conditions of a group of girls, productivity increased with each change (even when all the new-given privileges were removed).

The bank wiring room, where it was noted that a group at the front and one at the back were quite separate, although management hadn't specified this, and each had its norms and rules; and that each group had clear parameters, both upper and lower, for what they considered a fair day's work, and they had rules of their own to enforce it.

The main conclusions drawn from these studies (about 1930) were as follows:

— *Work is a group activity*, and people are not just pieces of soft machinery slotted together to perform work functions; nor are they separate individuals with no relationships with each other.

— *People like to feel special*, and having researchers or managers take an interest in their work and talk to them about it can affect the way they work.

— *There are informal groups in organizations*, which, though not specified (or even recognized) by management, have a strong influence on their members' work and performance.
— *Human relationships are a vital determinant of output*, both between one group member and the next, and between each subordinate and the boss.

Systems thinking

In the 1950s and 60s theorists turned their attention to the systematic similarities between organisms and machines, and sought to model the essential frameworks which made things survive and work in their environment. The basic open systems model is this (more elaborate in some textbooks):

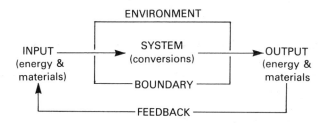

A business can be seen as a system, with raw materials, ideas, finance and work as the energy/materials input, the manufacturing process as the conversions, and the product, its advertising and PR, and wages and payments the output. Profits, market research and the Queen's Award to Industry are some of the feedback factors. Think all this through, and apply it to a simplified model of your bank.

Systems questions are rare in the examination, but the way of thought is helpful in structuring your view of organizations and useful in introductions to questions on OD (jargon for Organizational Design) questions.

Organization Behaviour, p. 250: Buchanan and Huczynski: Prentice Hall.

Contingency

This approach to looking at organization is, as its title suggests, that the design of an organization depends on that organization's circumstances. You will need to know about at least two and possibly three main 'theories': those of Burns and Stalker, of Joan Woodward and of Lawrence and Lorsch. Do read about them in full; but in essence, this is what they said:

Joan Woodward: The organization's structure depends on the way it makes its product — one-off, small batch, mass-production, continuous production. The fewer items made at a time, the 'shallower' the hierarchy and the more flexible the structures and the management thinking.

Burns and Stalker: Structure, type and attitudes adopted depend on the environment faced by the organization. There are two ideal types of organization to meet extremes of environments:

Organic (or organismic), facing a volatile, changing, unstable environment — such as advertising agencies or engineering companies making specialist items to individual specification. Such companies need to have a flexible structure, changing to meet the current demands, consulting rather than disciplinary.

Mechanistic, facing a stable, unchanging environment characterized by rules of procedure and stability. These are designed like the bureaucracy of Weber, with rules, hierarchies of control, and vertical authority and communication patterns — Government departments, for example.

The organization which has a structure not suited to the degree of volatility in its environment will not succeed.

Lawrence and Lorsch: The successful organization will in fact contain both types, indeed a range — the advertising department structured organically, the administration section mechanistically and so on. This is called 'differentiation'. To function, however, these departments must be coordinated by managers at a linking-pin position — this is called 'integration'. L & L's familiar diagrams look like this:

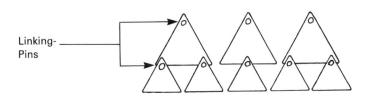

Linking-
Pins

Organizational design

Check this out in your textbooks. But know how to give an example of a traditional organizational chart, a 'concentric' or circular one, and a matrix structure, preferably trying these for your bank or division or department. Practise them in advance — don't make them up as you go along in the middle of your exam.

In fact, be prepared to draw diagrams at the drop of a hat: nothing helps to persuade the examiner that you are well-prepared and know your stuff than a neat, *accurate* and well-planned diagram.

Once you feel confident about your knowledge of this topic, try to answer the 10 multiple choice questions which follow.

Multiple choice questions

1 Which of the following are not characteristic of the rational/legal ideal type of organization:

   a hierarchy?
   b written records?
   c strong leadership?
   d qualified staff?

2 Which of the following defines a system as 'open':

   a vulnerability to environmental changes?
   b free and frank exchange of information between members?
   c interchange of input and output to and from the environment?
   d currently operating, none of its functions presently closed?

3 Which of the following is operated most closely by the branch banking system:

   a unit or one-off production?
   b batch operation?
   c mass-production techniques?
   d continuous-flow production?

4 The Hawthorne Experiments established, among other things, that:

   a work is a group activity, not just mechanical.
   b work conditions vitally determine people's output.
   c popular, friendly bosses are the most effective.
   d if left to themselves, people will set a low work rate.

5   The informal organization:

    a   arranges social events to keep staff happy.
    b   works out ways of working that management hasn't spotted.
    c   usually opposes what is officially proposed.
    d   sets standards and targets at the lowest possible level.

6   The 'Human Relations' approach to management:

    a   places importance on friendliness as a management trait.
    b   sets high performance standards and rewards accordingly.
    c   believes in consulting staff about job design.
    d   deals sympathetically with individual personal problems.

7   Which of the following characterizes staff management:

    a   concern with the production levels of a specific machine?
    b   solving company-wide information-flow problems?
    c   a belief that specialists are non-productive?
    d   handling disciplinary problems when they first arise?

8   Which of these quotes is from Tom Burns?

    a   'Production by the workers, the interests of the workers, the
        experiences and feelings of the workers: to these the leadership
        should pay constant attention"?
    b   'You may develop all the science that you please, and you may
        scientifically select and train workmen, just as you please, but
        unless some man or men bring the work together all your
        labour will be lost.'?
    c   'In peace there's nothing so becomes a man as modest stillness
        and humility: but when the blast of war blows in our ears, then
        imitate the action of the tiger. . . .'?
    d   'Mechanistic systems are, in fact, the 'Rational Bureaucracy' of
        an earlier generation of students of organisation. For the
        individual it provides an ordered world of work . . . . . within a

35

stable constellation of jobs, skills, specialised knowledge and sectional responsibilities.'?

9 Environment, control, boundaries, input/output, feedback: which of the following schools of organizational thinking is characterized by these concepts?

   a classical?
   b contingency?
   c feudal?
   d systems?

10 The best way of depicting an organization is:

   a with a traditional hierarchical chart.
   b on a matrix or grid-shaped chart.
   c concentrically, with the executive at the centre.
   d in a written prospectus.

Answers follow on pages 37-41. Score 2 marks for each correct answer.

Answers

1 The correct answer is **c**.

It is useful in this subject to have 'lists' in your mind, such as the characteristics of Bureaucracy, and to reproduce these lists perhaps as an introduction to your answers. Not all textbooks completely agree on the components of such lists (remember that the originals like Weber and Fayol wrote in languages which had to be translated, and some authors were struggling to simplify very complex concepts); so create and learn your own distillations of the textbook lists. Weber doesn't speak of *strong* leadership: the main characteristic is *appropriateness*. A person in a position which calls for leadership as part of its specification would be there because he/she would be *qualified* to be there and would arrive there by *prescribed hierachical routes*, and would be *trained* to perform the leadership task. Later in this volume we will distinguish between job-specification and person-specification: Weber spoke not of the character of people filling posts in the hierarchy, only of the job requirements.

2 The correct answer is **c**.

The word 'open' in 'open system' is a simple technical term which distinguishes it from 'closed': the former has openings in the boundary which allows it to interchange materials and energy with its environment, and the latter does not. All living systems, be they amoeba, people, organizations, football teams or the local corner shop are open systems. When looking at the design of organizations using systems thinking, it is useful to act as follows (a 'useful list'!):

— Specify organizational objectives.
— Define the boundary (not easy — in a bank, are the shareholders inside or out, and what about depositors' money?).
— Describe the environment and the types of input acquired and output produced by the system.
— Define and describe the conversion mechanisms, e.g. the decision system inside the larger system.
— Examine the ensuing design for ways of improving output, refining input, and affecting the feedback mechanisms in the environment.

3 The correct answer is **b**.

If, that is, there is a correct answer, because each of the production systems except, say, **d** is sometimes used: special funding for a major international project requiring a complex and unique repayment system would be one-off; much to the irritation of your Fathers in Banking, many of today's very useful consumer packages such as house insurance, or credit cards, or regular savings packages, could easily be described as mass-production. But batch-production, in which there are a number of repetitions of a single type of task, followed by a number of repetitions of a different one, should ring bells with you! At the risk of nagging you, do please look up what Joan Woodward said about these methods of production and how they affected management structure; and sit back and reflect on how your department or section or branch fits in to this way of thinking — before the examination...

4 The correct answer is **a**.

A vague, intuitive knowledge — which many managers have — of 'human relations' leads one to believe that this school of thought recommends being nice to people, asking them to do things instead of giving orders, providing social functions and being a good listener. In fact its central tenet is that understanding human interaction will give management better ways of using human resources. The Hawthorne Experiments clearly showed that human beings are not just pieces of manoeuvrable soft machinery, but that work is a group activity in which people like to feel special, and expert in what they do, and in which their relationships with each other and with management are important to them.

5 The correct answer is **b**.

For all the charts that organizations may draw, when people are assembled artificially into groups they will sort out for themselves, sometimes in parallel with and sometimes counter to the official view, groupings which suit their purposes, their need to associate (cf. Maslow, later in this volume). Such groupings create boundaries around themselves (specify who is in, who is out), have objectives and know what they want from the organization, have rules of member behaviour and ways of enforcing those rules, and set work levels which are 'proper': which means upper *and* lower levels, so that you may experience disapproval both for rate-busting or over-production and also for leadswinging and not pulling your weight. The informal group norms are by no means always opposed to the formal norms, but can conflict when the group's objectives are thwarted by the authorities. Quite often the informal group will spot ways of working which are an improvement on the official method, possibly because it suits the working people to operate in an easier or a simpler or a more personally satisfying or lucrative manner. Good management will not necessarily oppose the informal group or its leader, but will be aware of its identity and constitution, and may need to negotiate work practices rather than bulldoze them. An enormous amount of socio-psychological work has been done on group behaviour: use and apply the account you find in your textbooks to your work environment.

6 The correct answer is **c**.

Much of what can be said about this topic has been covered in the answer to Question 4; but not only did it come as something of a surprise to early researchers that people were concerned about, and possibly expert in, their own work: even now, 50 years later, there are managers who think so little of their workers' views that they will make changes at the workplace without any consultation. Those who do act in the true spirit of human relations do not do so from any charitable or condescending or altruitistic motive, but thereby utilize an important source of expertise, and also have a (possibly short-term but powerful) effect in terms of motivating those consulted. This is known as the 'Hawthorne Effect': while concentrating on the work as a result of being consulted, we produce more for a short time. True improvement, of course, comes from whatever changes in working practice arise out of our examination rather than the Hawthorne-Effect short-term increase in productivity.

7 The correct answer is **b**.

Examiners are annually amazed by the number of people who use the term 'staff management' in the context of this paper to mean personnel department. In organization theory it always means across-the-line specialist support to the direct producers of goods and services — and Personnel, and Computers, and the Dispatch Department, and the Administration Department, are all examples of staff sections. Examiners also abhor disparaging remarks about the net contribution of staff departments in banks, usually (of course) delivered by branch staff! It's like the mouth claiming that the stomach is an unnecessary parasite, 'whose wages we earn for them. . .'. Please note that the probability that your examiner is a staff manager is high! Seriously, be aware of the various functions of line and staff managers, thinking of the distinction in terms of a grid, with lines vertical and staff horizontal: branch and product departments are represented up and down the organization, and support sections across it. Reflect in advance of the exam on times where these departments work well together; about examples of possible conflict; and about practical ways of avoiding or solving conflict problems — for example a campaign carried out by bankers on the instructions of Marketing Department.

8   The correct answer is **d**.

First, look at the obvious clue: if you are familiar with Burns and Stalker you will have seen the word 'mechanistic', relating that to organic (or organismc) and the answer is then inevitable. Such buzzwords, all included in this chapter, must be second nature to you as you write your answers. *Second*, note that examiners seek clear evidence of study and, in this paper as in 'O' level English, to be able to quote — but genuinely, please — from the original author is always impressive; so collect and learn a few such quotes. *Third*, useful thoughts about management can come not just from your textbooks but from many different sources: *Banking World*, the *Financial Times*, television, such places as the sources quoted in this question. The answer to your next question are:

a Ex-Chairman Mao Tse-Tung: obviously a Human Relations man.
b F. W. Taylor.
c William Shakespeare: *Henry V*, the original Contingency Theorist. . .

9   The correct answer is **d**.

Hopefully by now that will be obvious to you. Note that systems thinking tends to be analytical rather than prescriptive: it is a way of looking at an organization, perhaps spotting communication or command bottlenecks, checking the nature of its relationship with its environment. The ways in which management should proceed are not of great interest to systems theorists; but you may be asked a question in which you feel inclined to use a system diagram to analyse a problem and make your own recommendations for action. For example: 'How would you go about improving the communication system of a branch where there have been difficulties in explaining new services to customers?' Remember that in this paper you are expected to have studied the nature of management and to apply what you have studied to the questions asked: in other words, to *think*!

10   There is no correct answer to this question: 2 marks if you said so.

Sorry — but in depicting an organization by means of a chart, or in words, the best way depends on the purpose to which the depiction is to be put. The traditional hierarchical chart has the advantage of familiarity; it indicates lines of authority and levels of seniority; it gives some idea of functions; and, to a limited extent, shows the interrelationships within and between departments. It doesn't usually show communication routes with any degree of clarity; it can be politically fraught; and it is static, not showing flows of energy, information and materials. The concentric diagram is almost identical in nature, except that it is unusual and might give a fresh view; it is less political, since precedence of one department over another is not even implied; and it is economical of space. The matrix or grid distinguishes line and staff functions, and is clear on communication and reporting lines, as well as indicating internally who is available to whom as an organizational resource; but it is rarely as simple as a straightforward grid, and usually has to be modified by numerous and sometimes complicated supplementary notes; and it is sometimes difficult — for those who care vitally about it — to know who is senior to whom. . .

Score 2 marks for each correct answer. What was your score for this topic? Fill it in on the score grid.

If you scored 12 or less and are still a bit shaky on some points go back and look at the study guide again, before proceeding any further.

If you are sure you really understand and are familiar with the topic now, try the 10 further questions which are on pages 164-166.

Alternatively you can go on to the next topic and do all the post-tests together at the end.

Topic 2   The Banking Environment

Study guide

There are certain basics in this topic; but the essence of it is *keeping up to date*. Good managers include in their skill the monitoring of the environment so that they can react to it, and it is this skill that the examiner is seeking here. So for good marks, it helps to revise by reading the business section of good newspapers, and watching TV programmes concerned with economic, social and technical matters, and maintaining a reasoned view of political developments.

In fact, for revision purposes, it helps to divide the topic into four areas: social, economic, political and technological environments.

The social environment

'What goes on in Society' doesn't change rapidly, except under special circumstances, such as war or revolution. But, as with all the headings in this chapter, you will need to be conscious of your social environment so as to be able to plan and cope with change — or anyway show the examiner that you can. Some of the topics you may need to be able to discuss will be:

— general social attitudes
— affluence and spending powers
— the employment situation
— attitudes to credit and its sources
— education
— the banks' competition

General social attitudes

Attitudes to work, to sex, to race can be isolated under this heading, although, as you may have found in other texts, there are many ways of dividing this chapter.

Don't be tempted to pontificate about the British Worker and his shovel on which he leans. Even today, most people want to be fairly paid for a fair day's *work*. There are, however, different attitudes to work depending on the person's time-horizon. People who have manual jobs do not think or plan in terms of a career, and do expect tangible short-term reward for extra work; whereas people in management adopt a longer time-horizon: give up present cash for future favour, do overtime free in the hope of promotion, do Grade 3 work when they are Grade 2 to prove they are worthy of advancement to Grade 3. Think about that and develop it.

Please take note of strong resistance to unemployment: most people don't like it, and press for the right to work — and beware the popular press notion that people prefer dole to work, which is patently untrue (more people earn less than they would if they went on the dole, than those who do that and claim benefits).

In our society, all are brought up to value the dignity of work, that what you do is your own, needed and valued. The work of Maslow and Herzberg can be applied here as well as in 'motivation' questions. But keep an eye on changing attitudes in the deprived areas like the inner cities.

One can almost put race and sex attitudes under the same heading, characterized perhaps by the phrase 'reducing but surviving prejudice'. The last fifteen years have seen great advancement in the views of society towards Asian and Afro-Caribbean people in management positions: but they are still rare. How many non-white branch managers do you know of? Women were accorded equal pay and rights in banks (to their credit) in 1967. Twenty years or so later, how many female branch managers are there in your bank? It would be genuinely useful for you to call your Personnel Department and ask them. Beware of the stock answers: 'They don't apply; they are hard to understand; they get pregnant and leave; they don't want careers'.

Before the exam., find and talk to (other) black people in your bank, and (other) females taking these exams, and debate the question of the advance of the less-privileged in work, and cooperate in noting the response.

Affluence

The idea of having a surplus of spending power over what you need to eat is not much more than 150 years old: nowadays we expect it. We spend money on consumer durables, on luxuries and on holidays. Our standard of living has improved, very steadily, since the late 40s. This alters the competitive situation in the market place but, more importantly in this section, it alters perception of what we can expect out of life. Carefully observe what worried governments always try and do nowadays: to reduce expectations if they can — and think about why that reduction might reduce inflation!

With increasing affluence (regardless of government efforts) comes increasing money movement: higher and more volatile deposits, much more cheque activity, very considerably grown account-holding — over 70% of the population have one sort of bank account or another, compared with nearer to 20% in the early 60's.

Employment

Take the trouble to know how employment — and unemployment — are measured, and what the up-to-date figures are at about exam-time. Store in your mind any examples you encounter of customers who become unemployed or redundant, and what in practice has happened on their account; look out for circulars giving advice on the matter.

Prepare in your mind your own carefully considered views on employment/unemployment and a sensible bank attitude to it; for instance bank involvement in Government initiatives in inner-city areas, such as Toxteth.

Attitudes to credit

It wasn't long ago that 'paying your way' was paramount. But credit is now tightly interwoven into our spending patterns, a fact acknowledged even by Marks & Spencer when they launched their own card in 1985. Note the move in banking to checking above all the ability to repay according to schedule (rather than as gone-concern); the increasing use of credit-scoring on customer rather than on the loan; the move towards unsecured lending; ingenious new schemes and accounts to tap the willingness of consumers to borrow; and new entrants to the credit market. Don't be tempted to take a moralistic attitude in the exam: the marker will be looking for a cool and dispassionate view.

Education

Note a current interest in making education a training for work; a felt need to standardize curricula; changing 'end' qualifications. Look out for using yourselves as typical examples: if you have four 'O' levels you're in the top (approximately) 15% of the population, the mean for which is nearer two CSEs, grade 2. By the way, with youth unemployment as high as it is, ask yourselves whether you still feel that a longer education is a good guarantee of good employment, and be prepared to discuss this.

Competition

It's not just the clearing banks, or even the building societies or insurance companies: it is *any* other way I can place money, borrow it or transmit it. Even spending money is competition if I might otherwise have deposited it.

List and think about competition for Deposits, Lending and Money Transmission: below, a 'start' for you:

Lending	Deposits	Transmission
Banks	Banks	Banks
Store cards	Building societies	Post Office
HP	Post Office	EFTPOS
Uncle James	A Rolls Royce	Take it yourself
	National savings	CHAPS, SWIFT

The economic environment

By this we usually mean the market and the competition's activities. Banks are no longer in a stable economic environment where traditional customers are looking for ordinary services from a comfortable organization serving their fathers before them. Customers are aware and discerning, price conscious and willing to switch (although the banks can still depend on some inertia). The market has changed; banks are now competitively different; and competition is now more widespread. Try to have a realistic idea of what your bank and others are up to in order to make a continuing profit.

The market

As previously mentioned, the personal market is increased. Computers have made it far more convenient for employers to pay wages through a bank, and easier for more customers to understand systems and make payments with non-cash methods; and to switch banks.

The business market is more sophisticated in banking practices and, as the economy has tightened, more discerning and particular about rates and commissions. Here, also, loyalty has ceased to be a paramount criterion for retaining a bank.

The banks

Within your living memory, banks were almost identical, offering almost exactly similar services, combining to arrange rates, and offering Mr Mainwaring of Warmington-on-Sea as the manager. They even advertised corporately, as evidenced by the 'Bank Manager in the Cupboard' campaign from which you may well still suffer.

Nowadays, a clerk moving from one bank to another would require time and effort to learn, not just new systems but also the range of services and account on offer. New corporate images and slogans abound. Before your exams, try asking your non-banking friends what they call to mind when the names of different clearing banks are mentioned (and discover something thereby about the effectiveness of advertising!)

Competition

This is coming from various directions. Interbank competition is now much fiercer, and the local bank managers' coffee mornings rarer. Until quite recently, taking a customer from another bank was called 'poaching' — implying illegality! Now it is called winning. . . . Reflect on whether your local management takes a modern view of competition.

Banks also have to compete with others previously excluded from their markets, such as store chains' credit cards, and in 1986 the advent of building societies into unsecured lending, insurance broking, chequebook and cash card accounts, and pensions finance, albeit as a modest percentage of their total assets, as yet.

As a result, advertising and promotional activities become more prominent; new and more convenient services appear; and bank staff are recruited and trained for different skills than their fathers in banking.

 Note — coolly and neutrally — what internal effect that has on staff motivation and development; think of examples of all this *in advance of the exams*, and be prepared to use them to illustrate points.

The political environment

Please remember that you are being marked by an examiner who, though guided by a schedule, in this subject is also allowed a measure of judgement. By the laws of nature (sometimes called 'X's Law'), if you reveal strong political *views*, as opposed to awareness, you will be marked by someone holding the opposite views, however, neutral they are supposed to be. Avoid any possible problem by exposing and expounding, but *not* supporting, political-environment points you need to make. It is hard to make you aware of what you need to know here, because by the time this is published, things will have changed: but keep an eye open on your run-up to the exams for:

— government attitudes towards nationalization/privatization
— schemes to encourage small businesses
— moves and changes in social security, pensions, health
— education and training policies, youth employment
— immigration, sex and equal opportunity legislation

— business and credit control

Read your newspapers, and the *Banking World*, in the run-up; watch TV programmes about business and society (a good excuse for relief from the books and notes occasionally); even listen to Radio 4 now and then.

The technological environment

Questions on this topic are *very* popular, in one form or another. Do prepare your answer to such questions, but remember to be flexible enough to adapt it to *answer the question*: examiners complain frequently about the misapplication of fairly good knowledge.

This is not the place to examine all the technological changes in banking, but structure your thinking about technology by sitting down and drawing a diagram. It might start by looking something like this:

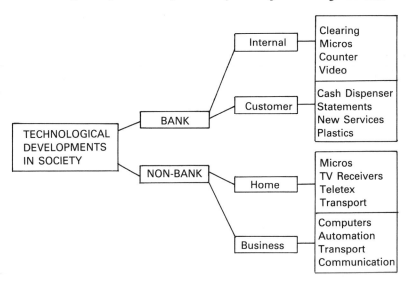

Do your own, if you like — doodle for an hour or two; prepare to be able to write a sentence or two under each heading; fix the whole thing in your mind; and in the exam, use those parts of it which fit the question. The diagram above, pleae note, is only a start to your revision process, and your own picture will be more effective for you.

Remember also that in this, as in any other question about the environment, you are taking an Institute of Bankers exam. 'What will be the effect on banking?' is often the tenor of the question. Really think about that, and answer straightforwardly and sensibly. The banks will not go out of existence; clerks will not disappear; the manager will probably still sit in the forbidding black chair; and society is now in fact more cashful than when, fifteen years ago, the cashless society was supposed to be upon us.

But there will be changes, and your career is proceeding right into the heart of them. So think realistically about what they may be, with that very personal thought in mind!

Once you feel confident about your knowledge of this topic, try to answer the 10 multiple choice questions which follow.

Multiple choice questions

1 Which of the following is not a demographic factor important in people's attitudes to each other:

a race?
b sex?
c musical taste?
d age?

 *answer*

2 Which of these is not directly competitive with clearing banks as the taker of personal deposits:

a building societies?
b merchant banks?
c SAYE schemes?
d the Post Office?

 *answer*

3 Which of the following is an important principle in Conservative Party policy:

a free National Health services?
b tax-free business expenses?
d widespread share-ownership?
d progressive personal taxation?

 *answer*

4 Which of the following cannot be obtained from either a branch or a specialist section of a UK clearing bank:

a credit cards?
b acceptance credit?
c eurocurrency dealing and advice?

   d hire purchase finance?

5 Which of these may you one day find at a supermarket till:

   a EPOS?
   b EXPO?
   c EFTPOS?
   d EFTA?

6 About what proportion of the population currently holds a bank account of one sort or another:

   a 70%?
   b 50%?
   c 25%?
   d 10%?

7 What is the average educational attainment of the UK adult:?

   a two CSEs?
   b two 'O'-levels?
   c four 'O'-levels?
   d one 'A'-level?

8 Which of the following is not controlled directly by the banks (and you may like to revise what they stand for):

   a BACS?
   b CHAPS?
   c SWIFT?
   d EXTEL?

9 Which of the following phrases does not refer to recent legislation:

    a health and safety at work?
    b equal opportunities for men and women?
    c government spending on national infrastructure?
    d protection of employment in maternity?

answer

10 Which of these items of software is not universally useful to a small business using a microcomputer for its administration:

    a CAD?
    b spreadsheet programmes?
    c word-processing packages?
    d databases?

answer

Answers on pages 52-54. Score 2 marks for each correct answer.

Answers

1 The correct answer is **c**.

Your taste in music may be important in your attitude towards others, and if you 'support' Queen, or Status Quo, or Johann Sebastian Bach this can colour your views of people who are fans of others. But it is not directly a demographic factor, which are matters of vital statistics illustrating the nature of communities; while the sex, age and racial breakdown of that community are such factors.

2 The correct answer is **b**.

Merchant banks use investors' money rather than depositor's assets in financing loans, usually to organizations. Clearly banks, building societies, SAYE schemes and the Post Office do take deposits; and clearing banks and building societies give the depositor a return and use assets of which they are custodian, not usually owner, to lend to others.

3 The correct answer is **c**.

The Conservatives do believe in the provision and promotion of a *subsidised* health service, but not free except to those who cannot afford it at all, and with fees at higher income levels, and harmonized with a significant private sector; they are perfectly happy to tax business expenses; they believe that progressive taxation, harsher as income rises, discourages private and managerial enterprise; and claim to wish to reduce taxation.

They do encourage widespread share ownership and have instituted savings and profit-sharing share-purchase tax-concessions schemes, not to mention 'privatization', to further this end.

4 The correct answer is **none of them**.

If you said 'none of them', give yourself 2 marks: one (grudging) mark for choosing any one of the suggested services, since clearing banks in the UK offer all these services. You should be familiar with the services provided by your own (or any) clearing bank. One way of doing this is to look at the leaflets and other literature provided by the bank to the public: have you ever done that? — it's excellent revision.

5 The correct answer is **c**.

You won't find EXPO, which isn't relevant at all and is short for 'exhibition'; the European Free Trade Association is to be found elsewhere; something of a trick question in that EPOS — Electronic Point-of-Sale systems — are *already* to be found in supermarkets, where bar-codes are read by laser projectors, and you can give yourself a half-mark for that; but EFTPOS, Electronic Fund-Transfer at Point of Sale, has not yet been introduced except at a very experimental level, needing as it will the entire agreement of banks and retailers.

6 The correct answer is **a**.

Growth in bank account holdings has been enormous in the last fifteen years, since radical computerization programmes in the early 1970s. The biggest factor was the demand for efficient payroll systems, requiring employees to have wages and salaries paid into a bank account — not just the manager of the hotel but also the floor housekeeper; not just the canteen manager but also the assistant domestic.

7 The correct answer is **a**.

This is not a condemnation of the education system, just a matter of setting an average standard. Two CSEs (actually at less than Grade 1) is *defined* as educationally average; the usual minimum for bank clerks' entry is four 'O'-levels, and this puts you into the top approximately 17–20%.

8 The correct answer is **d**.

EXTEL is a private company which provides company information. BACS is the Bankers' Automated Clearing Service; CHAPS is Clearing House Automated Payments System; and SWIFT is Society for Worldwide Interbank Financial Telecommunications.

9 The correct answer is **c**.

Unless policies change, spending on the national infrastucture (sewers, roads, national buildings, derelict spaces) is not even a government priority, never mind a subject of recent legislation. If they *do* change, you should know about it, because reading national newspapers — the news and financial sections — is good practice for a banker and good revision for this exam.

10 The correct answer is **a**.

CAD stands for Computer-Aided Design, and is useful only to businesses which deal in or are dependent on efficient graphic design. Spreadsheets are matrices or grids of information, in which you can manipulate mathematically any one box with any other — useful in preparing accounts, cash-flows, forecasts; word-processors are advanced typewriter/storage-retrieval/editing systems; and databases are electronic card-index-type storage and retrieval systems for listed information. All of the last three are by their nature useful to any small business.

Score 2 marks for each correct answer. What was your score for this topic? Fill it in on the score grid.

If you scored 12 or less and are still a bit shaky on some points go back and look at the study guide again, before proceeding any further.

If you are sure you really understand and are familiar with the topic now, try the 10 further questions which are on pages 166-168.

Alternatively you can go on to the next topic and do all the post-tests together at the end.

Topic 3   Managerial Roles and Processes

Study guide

While you will sometimes get questions about managerial role and/or processes in the case-study form ('Advise Jim Smith how he should see himself in his new role as Assistant Manager of Petrograd Branch. . . .'), direct questions on this topic are quite popular. The Institute justfiably sees this subject as fairly central to this paper.

It is one which ought to be popular, if only because you can memorize 'lists' of headings under which you need to elaborate briefly. A good deal of current thinking and writing is going on in this area at the moment, and unlike some other topics in which the 'classics' were established in the past, some newer models are becoming accepted as textbook favourites and you and your mentors (lecturers or books) must keep up to date.

You need to be careful, because if the question uses such phrases as 'the role of the manager', that must not be confused with 'management style', or 'leadership'. Your examiners take a firm line when it comes to what are roles and what are the conventionally accepted managerial processes; equally they admire firm and confident answers.

Even within the role field there are several subject areas which appear acceptable in answers, and we shall deal with them in this chapter under the subheadings of:

1 Role
   1.1 Concepts
   1.2 Managerial roles
   1.3 Management team roles
2 Management tasks and processes

Role

Role concepts

Role itself is not a simple concept: but you can recognize an organizational or social role usually because it has a label or name, like

55

'Father' or 'Boss' or 'Securities Clerk' or 'Commuter'. It is a collection of rights, duties, tasks, language, dress and appropriate behaviour, so that when you are being, say, 'Lecturer', people recognize that and can tell whether you are doing it correctly, and can react to your behaviour correctly in their role.

Role requirements are what determines what is correct role behaviour, from outside the role. A job-description is a set of formal role requirements; but often there are informal requirements too, for example how language is used: the role of 'Bank-Manager' doesn't call for strongly-worded abuse, while the same person on the terraces at Old Trafford in the 'Football-Fan' role using emphatic words would not seem out of place.

Role expectations are the role-holder's views on how the role should be taken. They usually coincide with the requirements; but if not, they can lead to instability in the situation (imagine the 'Bank Manager' shouting 'Yellow Card' at a customer who has overdrawn without permission. . . .).

Role conflict arises when two or more contradictory roles are indicated: 'I'm my son's boss, he breaks company rules: bosses fire people who do that, fathers don't deprive sons of their livelihood'. Or 'I'm a bank manager and my best friend's chance of business success depends on a loan on a clearly a high-risk proposition: bankers don't make such loans, friends don't hesitate'. Handling role conflict depends on access to exit from the situation, or successful role separation by the role(s) holder.

Role ambiguity is when two contradictory behaviours are required in the same role: 'be curious, ambitious, show initiative', on the one hand; and 'what are you doing rummaging about in those customer files, get on with your filing' on the other.

The *role set* are all the interconnecting roles which interact or are supposed to interact with the *focal role*. It is quite interesting to draw spidery rambling diagrams of the role set: try it with your job-role in the centre, and move out.

Finally (though there are more, but this will become a sociology text book if we're not careful), there are *role signs*, which make it evident, or by which role-holders intend to make it evident, that they are in role: such as uniforms, like policemen's helmets or pin-stripe suits, or special phrases — only bankers 'undertake a comprehensive review of your financial situation' meaning 'see how you're fixed for money', and 'grant you facilities in the way of advances' meaning 'Lend you the cash'.

All this will act as background for what follows. You will have noted that I can have a number of roles, no two of which I actually occupy at one time, although they can overlap a bit: I am lecturer, writer, father, fellwalker, boss, colleague, friend and so on. The same goes for managerial roles.

Organisational Behaviour, p. 335: Buchanan and Huczynski: Prentice Hall.

Managerial roles

This is based on the work of Henry Mintzberg, writing in the early 1970s and well enough established to form the basis of an acceptable answer. He contends that there are *in fact* (based on research into what top managers actually do) ten managerial roles under three headings. *Learn this*:

Interpersonal roles	Informational roles	Decisional roles
Figurehead	Monitor	Entrepreneur
Leader	Disseminator	Disturbance Handler
Liaison	Spokesman	Resource allocator
		Negotiator

This is an elaboration of the above headings. As you read each one, think of specific things that your manager does within each role description:

Interpersonal roles

Figurehead: Ceremonial duties, attending social functions on behalf of the group, hosting important visitors.

Leader: Motivation, training, and counselling the subordinate; recruiting, replacing and staffing levels.

Liaison: Establishing and maintaining network of useful contacts outside the group.

Informational Roles

Monitor: Seeks and receives information from inside and outside the group, to monitor progress. Acts as 'nerve-centre'.

Disseminator: Provides information to members of the group and the organization, with interpretation if necessary.

Spokesman: Transmits information to people outside the organization; acts as expert on organization/industry.

Decisional roles

Entrepreneur: Seeks out opportunities within and outside organization;

initiates/designs improvement projects.

Disturbance Handler:	Monitors unusual or disturbance situations; initiates actions to resolve or correct them.
Resource Allocator:	Allocates all organizational/group resources, material, people, time: in fact, all vital organizational decisions.
Negotiator:	Represents the group in internal and the organization in external negotiations.

Understanding Organisations, p. 363: Handy: Penguin.

Management team roles

A more recent account of roles in management has been suggested by Belbin who says that individual managers alone are less effective in solving continuing business problems than a well-constructed team; and that team would include the following roles, possibly at times combined in one individual, though some people are better suited to one than another:

Chairman:	A judge and balanced thinker, coordinates team efforts with disciplined organizational thinking.
Shaper:	The outgoing, creative, dominant, driving person: a well-spring of emotional energy, leads on specific tasks.
Plant:	Intellectual and imaginative, provides many of the ideas for direction and progress; but quiet, needs drawing out.
Monitor-Evaluator:	The logical evaluator of ideas, the analyser of the group's creative progress, dissector of arguments.
Resource-Investigator:	Monitor of outside information, liaison and contact; sociable, public-relations oriented, popular and relaxed.
Company Worker:	The useful bureaucrat and administrator, keeps the charts and timetables up to date; the efficient team member.
Team Worker:	Quietly works within the team, promoting harmony, resolving conflict, ensuring smooth team relationships.
Finisher:	The one who drives, nags and cajoles the group to meet deadlines, beat controls, get the job done in time.

An effectve team contains all of these; the best person to fill the role is the one best fitted emotionally; too many of the same emotional-intellectual type, or missing types, unbalances the team.

 Understanding Organisations, p. 165: Handy: Penguin.

Management processes

Your examiner consistently sees the management process — a series of essential responsibilities that the manager must take as the world of business progresses — as divided under six headings, which you should *learn*, as follows:

1 Setting objectives   4 Organization and coordination
2 Forecasting   5 Motivation
3 Planning   6 Control

Setting objectives: Vital if the direction of the unit is not to be awry, and setting the yardstick against which planning and control are measured. Objectives must not only be set but communicated to the group.

Forecasting: Estimating what likely trends there are, internally and in the environment, for example market directions and growth, to set the background as accurately as possible for the planning, organizing and control processes.

Planning: Sometimes developing longer term (5–10 year) plans for the direction of the enterprise, and always medium and shorter term plans for specific action, often concrete and quantifiable, but flexible enough to accommodate adjustments as forecasts alter.

Organization and coordination: Making sure that the structure and functions of the group are geared to carry out the plans and achieve the objectives: the 'present tense' of planning.

Motivation: Worthy of special attention in itself, and a complete chapter in this book. Suffice it to relate it here to the other processes because they cannot work without the commitment of people, which itself demands constant vigilance, attention and action on the part of the manager, as well as development, guidance, encouragement and orientation towards organizational goals.

Control: Obtaining information, and setting timed and planned stages, to see to it that the planning and organization is on path, and monitoring and adjusting progress towards the objectives.

These processes are more difficult to observe in action, and it is harder for you to conjure up examples of them at work, mainly because their manifestations are not always made explicit to staff, and they are usually considered and discussed at higher level; but also because they are not always well done in modern business, if we are to be realistic.

On a warning note, with reference to that last comment: it is in the context of this topic that it is tempting to be cynical in your examination answers about your own management branch or bank. While examples of management practice in action are welcomed, nevertheless the examiners are never happy about sarcasm or complaints. They don't want what we might call 'Barclaymoan', even if they do like factual evidence for reasoned observations illustrating points of theory or principle.

Finally, a reminder that in case-study-style questions, always state the principle and then apply it to the circumstances or characters outlined in the case, to show that you have studied and are taking a systematic approach, rather than hitting on correct solutions by instinct or chance.

Once you feel confident about your knowledge of this topic, try to answer the 10 multiple choice questions which follow.

Multiple choice questions

1 A role is, most closely:

    a a part in a play.
    b a position in a bank.
    c a substitute for your personality.
    d a set of expected behaviours.

2 Which of the following is one of Belbin's 'team roles':

    a shaper?
    b fixer?
    c minder?
    d pusher?

3 Which of these describes role ambiguity:

    a conflicting feelings about a role?
    b more than one role occuring simultaneously?
    c conflicting demands within the same role?
    d no clarity as to which role to adopt?

4 Which of the following is a Decisional role, in Mintzberg's model:

    a monitor?
    b negotiator?
    c leader?
    d liaison?

5 One of these is not normally seen to be part of the managerial process:

    a administrating.
    b planning.
    c controlling.
    d forecasting.

answer

6 The 'Monitor-Evaluator':

    a is a useful bureaucrat, gets things in shape, organized.
    b provides intellectual ideas for progress, is the thinker.
    c obtains information and contacts from outside the group.
    d evaluates ideas, analyses the work, logically dissects.

answer

7 One of the following is not a role-sign:

    a a policewoman's uniform.
    b a banker's AIB tie.
    c a footballer's shinpads.
    d a Sainsburys shop assistant's uniform.

answer

8 What is a focal role:

    a the role from which a role-set is drawn up?
    b the most important person in a role-set?
    c the role regarded as the leader-role in a role-set?
    d the role that most members of the role-set interact with?

answer

9 Which of these is *planning* as opposed to forecasting:

    a anticipating future trends on the basis of past events?
    b setting up actions to cope with future events?
    c extrapolating data to provide expectations?

d examining probabilities as to the short, medium and long term?

answer

10 Choose the best description of *motivation* from the list below:

    a getting people to do what the organization wants them to do.
    b getting them to do what they want to do.
    c getting them to want to do what the organization wants.
    d getting them to do what you want them to do.

answer

Answers follow on pages 64-66. Score 2 marks for each correct answer.

Answers

1 The correct answer is **d**.

Certainly a part in a play is called a role, and it is from the dramatic sense of role that social science has taken the name. In a play, the actor's character and personality are not relevant when playing the role, except if parts of them are deliberately used to contribute to the way the role is played. A position in a bank is also a role, but only one type of role. Role is not a substitute for personality, certain aspects of which may have to be suppressed, however, in certain roles. In fact, a role is defined by the behaviours expected of anyone assuming it.

2 The correct answer is **a**.

Belbin's other roles will be found in the study guide for this topic. To remind you, they are:

Chairman	Resource Investigator
Shaper	Company Worker
Plant	Team Worker
Monitor-Evaluator	Finisher

If you got this answer wrong, don't just award yourself no points: go back and look the team roles up — memorize the list and their characteristics!

3 The correct answer is **c**.

Don't confuse the conflicting demands within a role with conflicting roles. Teachers have to deal with role *ambiguity* in balancing how much they help students (as Teacher they are supposed to help them) with how much they leave to the students to discover for themselves (as Teacher they are supposed to do that too). They have to deal with role *conflict* when they have relationships of family or friendship with their students, and enjoy their company as Friend or Mother, and yet have to punish them as Teacher.

4 The correct answer is **b**.

Figure, Leader and Liaison are interpersonal roles; Monitor, Disseminator and Spokesman are informational roles; it is Negotiator, along with Entrepreneur, Resource Allocator and Disturbance Handler, which are the decisional roles. Check back to the study guide and look at the definitions if you got this wrong, or if you *guessed* right. . .

5 The correct answer is **a**.

Administration is important, but it isn't managerial. A manager manages administrators, among others: they simply keep records, keep the books in order, carry out mechanical requests, keep things tidy. A manager should be involved in a wide range of decisional activities. Do make sure you know the elements of the managerial process as outlined here and in the study guide: it is a frequent and favourite topic of the examiners, and quite justifiably so. They are:

Setting objectives
Forecasting
Planning
Organization and coordination
Motivation
Control

6 The correct answer is **d**.

You'll have recognized a Belbin term, of course. . . The person who gets the team into shape and organized is the Shaper; intellectual ideas and thinking come from the Innovator; it is the Resource Investigator who has contact with and gets information from outside the group; and the Monitor-Evaluator checks out internal information and analyses data and conclusions drawn therefrom.

7 The correct answer is **c**.

Shinpads are useful, possibly indispensible, but they are functional rather than a display of status or role, unlike the colours and pattern of the football socks which cover them, which say, 'I play for Metropole United', or the policewoman's uniform, or the AIB tie, or the Sainsbury overall (which is only a role-sign because of its distinctive colour and pattern, and not its function).

8 The correct answer is **a**.

When describing or depicting a role set, it is the focal role that the role set belongs to, i.e. whose role set you are describing or depicting. This is a bit technical; the others can be a focal role if you happen to be concentrating on them and drawing up the role set of the most important person, or the leader, or the frequent interacter.

For example, if the focal role is Teenage Vegetarian Daughter, then there are Father, Mother, Sister, Health-food Shop Owner, ASDA's Supermarket Management, other Vegetarian Contemporaries, Omnivorous Contemporaries, other Concerned Relatives, Members of other Alternative-Culture Groups and so on. Each of these could be the focal role if it is *their* role set you want to describe.

9 The correct answer is **b**.

It is simple in that it follows the colloquial usage — which isn't always the case with social science terms. Forecasting has to do with foretelling future *situations*, as in anticipating, extrapolating and examining probabilities. Planning refers to intended *actions* to deal with those situations. You can't plan without forecasting, but you can forecast without planning.

10 The correct answer is **c**.

If all four answers coincide how wonderful! This is because congruency between organization, managerial and individual motivation means no motivational problems. Look out for confusion between **c**, getting them to want to do things, tapping their internal motivation, and **d**, getting them to do things, which anyone in a position of power can do by force or bribery or threat. This is not motivation, though there exist managers who think it is — ever met one?

Score 2 marks for each correct answer. What was your score for this topic? Fill it in on the score grid.

If you scored 12 or less and are still a bit shaky on some points go back and look at the study guide again, before proceeding any further.

If you are sure you really understand and are familiar with the topic now, try the 10 further questions which are on pages 169-171.

Alternatively you can go on to the next topic and do all the post-tests together at the end.

Topic 4 Managerial Techniques and Tools

Study guide

This rather idiosyncratically named section of the syllabus covers a number of subjects on which the examiners like to ask questions, perhaps partly because they can be systematically (i.e. with good solid lists of subheadings) answered, examined and marked.

They can therefore be systematically — by the above definition — learnt, though with a little time to go before your exam, you should not only learn the lists but also be ready with examples under each heading thought out *in advance*; with an understanding of what you are saying which you are prepared to demonstrate; and with a sensible flexibility so that you can apply what you know to the exact requirements of the straight question, or to the facts of the case-study question.

The syllabus writer makes a particular point of saying in the Regulations, Syllabus and Tuition Guide (you *have* read that, surely, haven't you?) that 'A detailed knowledge of the techniques is not required'. By that you may assume that they require knowledge of the bare mechanism, but mainly of the use and applications of the techniques involved; so questions on these topics are often of the case-study type.

There are a variety of topics mentioned in the syllabus, and the list is extended and/or varied in your textbooks, the appropriate chapter in which you should check out. You are well advised to have a small armoury of them in the form of lists (you'll see what I mean as you read on). Those we will deal with here are:

1 Market and consumer research
2 Attitude surveys
3 Decision making
4 Problem solving
5 Planning, forecasting, budgets, critical path and MbO.

Market and consumer research

Market research

The examiners, rightly concerned about the internal aspects of competent management, don't often ask questions about the market; but the sort of techniques described here can be used to check out and obtain evidence for the solution of internal problems. To investigate a market you need to:

1. *Segment*: find out, or define for yourself, who your market is. The market for your bank's banking services is *not* every member of the public, but those with incomes; not all of those, but those who are not criminal; not all of those, but those who are, say, not employees of other banks; and not all of those but those whose accounts are likely to be profitable to your bank.
2. *Set objectives*, asking what the research is for, what facts or opinions you need and about what and from whom.
3. *Select methodology* for collecting and analysing data: questionnaire (postal, personal, telephone?), desk or library research, consumer research, computer-based techniques.
4. *Collect data* — carefully and in the planned form, without variations, so that the analysis is valid.
5. *Analyse data*, with an eye on the objectives, seeing to it that the analysis is aimed at giving you the needed information.
6. *Present* comment (the evidence), conclusions (the verdict) and recommendations (the sentence) for the efficient consumption of those who will make marketing decisions based on the research.

Consumer research

The same chronological process, but concerned with some or all of the following facts about your consumers directly, and obtained by *field research* (asking them) or *desk research* (checking out library, government, local authority or market research bureau data):

their number — how many are there?
their demographics — class, sex, age, race, religions
their location — where do they live, work, play, eat?
their buying habits — how do they decide?
                      who decides?
                      how often and how much do they buy?
their needs — what do they want the service for?
              what do they want it to do?
              where and when do they want it available?

their spending expectations — how much will they pay for it?
their image of it — what opinions of existing services?
their aspirations — what do they think the ideal service is?

Attitude surveys

Oddly, the examiners seem quite keen on these. Often in their reports on certain case-study questions it is suggested that personnel departments or regional/area management can find out about why so many Samantha's and Conrad's are taking irregular sick-leave by putting about a staff questionnaire or performing an internal attitude survey. It would be interesting to know if this technique is used with any regularity, if at all, in the real world.

Still, if it is popular in answers, then it is sensible to be systematic in reproducing your knowledge thereof.

Attitude surveys are usually done by written questionnaire, carefully designed for some of these questions and factors:

What do we want to know?
What questions must we therefore ask?
How do we avoid confusion in those questions?
How do we avoid bias in the answers?
How many do we need to do to get a good sample?
How can we get people to fill in and return the questionnaires?
What are we going to do with the answers?

As a revision exercise, carefully think through commonsense answers to these questions in the context of an attitude survey to discover reasons for low morale in one area or region of your bank.

Often in this type of question the examiner expects you to say that the investigator, looking at low morale or increased sick-leave or absenteeism or labour turnover, should supplement the survey with:

Careful statistical analysis, including
   comparisons with non-affected areas
   comparisons with past-period records for the same area
Personal interviews with a random sample of staff
Personal interview with affected staff
Check of central appraisal records if accessible
Personal interviews with local management
Visits to the affected area

Learn these lists; add to them; where appropriate, think of examples in advance of your examination, remembering that revision is supposed to be an active, thinking activity!

Decision making

A classic topic in which, either in case-study or in straight questions, you can state the principle (in the form of a list) and apply it to the details of the question, thus proving to the examiner that you have studied, and can also apply the theory in a managerial and practical manner as befits an AIB. . .

The 'list' in this case is of the steps to be gone through in the ideal decision, and usually reads something like this:

Need: discern the need for a decision to be made
Criteria: calculate criteria for a 'good' decision
Facts: collect relevant facts and opinions
Analysis: analyse facts using tools, technology
Alternatives: set forth all alternative courses of action
Utilities: attach a value to each, given criteria
Probabilities: attach probability of success to alternatives
Calculate optimum course of action (Utility × Probability)
Forecast side-issue outcomes to best decisions
Select course of action
Implement; Communicate; Monitor

Before you go on to the next section, and before you memorize this list, apply it:

First, to the decision concerning what we are going to do for entertainment this Saturday evening.

Then, to which of the City Centre branch staff should be permitted to use the newly available single space in the branch car park.

You will probably find that not every one of the steps apply, but the model does largely seem to work, and if there is a question to which you can apply it systematically you can pick up good marks.

Sometimes there is a reference to *group* decision making as opposed to *individual* decision making. You can take the above model and look at which steps are better done by a group than by an individual, and vice-versa; and you can expand on the thought that groups can be more *powerful* at generating alternative courses of action, and in implementation, but individuals are always *faster*, and usually less expensive in time and personal resources.

You can also refer in such a question to responsibility in decision making, bringing in models of management style which include

Consultative (manager consults staff before making decisions) and Participative (group makes decisions, manager organizes implementation).

Problem solving

There are clear, in fact remarkable, similarities between problem solving, in theory, and decision making, and the examiner can decide to ring changes by asking about the former. The problem solving process can be depicted as follows:

Recognize the existence of a problem
Criteria: set out criteria for a good solution
Facts: collect relevant facts and opinions
Analysis: analyse facts in terms of problem
Alternatives: examine all alternative solutions
Value-calculation of alternative solutions, in terms of criteria
Selection of most valuable solution
Implement, Communicate, Monitor
Remain sensitive to existence of new problems

Again, as a revision exercise, apply this model of the procedural steps to:

First, the chip-pan having suddenly burst into flames.

Then, the discovery that young Anna, having been put on the counter to serve as a cashier, is extremely miserable because she actually urgently desired to be a terminal operator.

Planning, forecasting, objectives etc.

There are miscellaneous techniques of management which either are specifically referred to in a question, or which will get you marks if you apply them sensibly. Some of the most prominent of these are planning, forecasting and budgetary control, critical path analysis, and mangement by objectives. These we outline below.

'Lumped together' in the syllabus, what they seem to have in common is that they are logical techniques using quantitative or systematic methods; they are familiar to all who have had management education; and they are rarely if ever seen in action in the real world. . .

By all means become familiar with those dealt with here, and add one or two more to your collection before the exams. Be able to explain the basics, and be ready to apply them ingeniously to the question you may be asked.

Planning and forecasting

. . . Or rather, the other way round: forecasting is making educated suppositions about how the future will be, and planning is making decisions in advance as to future actions. You can't plan without forecasting.

Forecasting is usually done using the past as a base, establishing trends and extrapolating (good word) into the future. This is most easily done graphically, and can be done on any scale from wide, national economic statistics right down to local-branch absenteeism figures. The forecaster lays out the past, factual trend figures; makes explicit assumptions based on known, and then additionally supposed future changes in the environment, and in the object of the forecast; and draws up the forecast figures, graphs or statements.

Planning is very often associated in the textbooks, and in exam answers, either with 'range' or 'level', and these seem also to be closely related: there are long, medium and short range plans, and there are also corporate, strategic, middle level management and operational (or ground level) plans. Do take a little time now to understand these in common-sense terms, and if you can apply *both* of these concepts to question, your answer will look good.

Remember for an extra mark or two that good forecasts and plans are *flexible*, taking into account on a *rolling* basis actual changes in the planning object and the environment, and being *adjusted* accordingly. This is preferably completely *continuous*, but should at least be *frequent*, *periodic* and/or *regular* (all good 'planning' words).

Budgets and budgetary control

Budgets are not so much plans as planned future constraints: the financial/resource limits within which those budgeted must work. If your bank has a budget system, look at it as a revision exercise.

Budgets are for outgoings or expenditure and also incomings or income. They set standards of (usually) quantitative performance, the *expected*, and they look to accurate *record keeping* of the *actual*. The difference is usually called the *variance*, sometimes expressed as a percentage as well as absolute, and there are often either-side permitted limits, such as with marketing targets.

Most importantly, there should be a mechanism for *explanation of variance* at regular intervals shorter than the whole budget period, so that the budgeter, or the budgeted, can take *corrective action* either instantaneously or at the end of the budget period as a result of the *periodic review* (use the buzzwords — remember what you are sitting in the exam-room trying to prove to the examiner).

Critical path analysis

This is the most popularly quoted of the two main *network analysis* techniques, the other being PERT (Program Evaluation Review Technique). It is a graphic, usually computerized technique for working out how long a project will take, and when and in what order the various elements need to be started.

A frequently used non-work example is cooking a meal: each element is started at different times so that all are ready at the correct moment, and you can imagine drawing the diagram, starting from the meal-time and working backwards to the point at which the first action (peel the potatoes?) needs to be taken.

Try that now as a revision exercise — don't take more than a few minutes though.

You can also imagine, having drawn the first draft, how that diagram can be redrawn and adjusted for better efficiency; and how a computer program designed to do just that would be effective.

Now think of that process, say, for building a house; or, more relevantly, for the launch of a new bank service, including setting marketing targets, briefing staff, producing procedural or manual material, advertising literature, TV or press advertisements, financial and accounting set-ups, training, designing, approving, and printing forms, vouchers and other documentation, getting legal clearance and so on.

Like many another sensible technique, it isn't often manifestly used: but, apart from the exam, you may find it useful even if informally to plan projects at work — or at home.

Management by objectives

Here's another technique more spoken of in AIB exams than seen in action, although many would agree with the underlying principles, and you can often observe it used on an informal basis between managers of one and a subordinate level. You may get a casual mark by mentioning the fathers of MbO (its usual abbreviation), namely Peter Drucker and John Humble.

Essentially it is a formal managerial process in which targets are set up for the individual manager's performance, which is reviewed, corrected and rewarded against those targets. It is part of the philosophy that the relationship between the manager and the boss is cooperative and supportive, and that the manager is willing and motivated to participate (marks for this too).

Therefore, *by manager and boss* in collaboration (very important):

The *job definition*, and limits of authority and control are agreed
Objectives for the job are generally defined
Key areas are defined in which results are to be achieved
Standard of performance appropriate to the job are agreed
Flexibility is built in for contingencies/unforeseens
Resources and budgets are agreed, and any necessary *training*
Monitoring and communication systems are set up
Performance review is regular and frequent
Reward is directly linked to achieving objectives

Learn this, and any other of the lists in this chapter that appeal to you. Listen carefully — I will say this only once (more): *Read the question carefully, discern which management technique the examiner wants you to apply, produce your intelligently expanded list, and apply it sensibly and practically to the details of the question.*

Once you feel confident about your knowledge of this topic, try to answer the 10 multiple choice questions which follow.

Multiple choice questions

1 Dividing a market up so as to define the part you are specifically aiming at is called:

   a sectioning.
   b seccoteuring.
   c segmenting.
   d selecting.

2 In which of the following ways is a market research questionnaire not normally administered:

   a by post?
   b by telephone?
   c in person?
   d on noticeboards?

3 One of the following is not a demographic factor:

   a income.
   b sex.
   c race.
   d age.

4 Which of these characterizes *individual* as opposed to *group* decision making:

   a it is fast?
   b it is cumbersome?
   c it is accurate?
   d it is expensive?

5 Before going about solving a problem you must:

   a determine who is responsible.
   b recognize its existence.
   c look at alternative solutions.
   d prepare yourself mentally.

 _answer_

6 One of the following does not describe usual actions in budgetary control systems:

   a explanation of variance.
   b periodic review.
   c corrective action.
   d monetary reward.

 _answer_

7 PERT stands for:

   a Program Evaluation Review Technique.
   b Program Exercise in Reaction Technique.
   c Programmed Evaluation and Revision Technique.
   d Personal Evacuation and Relaxation Technique.

 _answer_

8 Which of these is the critical path in a project:

   a the longest individual action.
   b the shortest inevitable set of actions.
   c the longest necessary set of actions.
   d the most important set of actions.

 _answer_

9 Peter Drucker is one of the authors of the technique known as:

   a management science.
   b management by objectives.
   c management by exception.

d management development.

answer

10 Planning concerns itself principally with:

    a forecast future events.
    b the short term future.
    c the medium term future.
    d the long term future.

answer

Answers follow on pages 78-80. Score 2 marks for each correct answer.

Answers

1 The correct answer is **c**.

The others have no relevance to marketing. It is the first sign of a reasonably sophisticated marketer — and examination candidate — to segment the market according to need, income, social situation, locality etc., rather than naively believing that all the public is a market for any product: that is true only of such basic life-essentials as salt, water, energy.

2 The correct answer is **d**.

It is possible to put a questionnaire up on a noticeboard, but the results would not be as effective as the others, where the choice of respondant and/or the supervision of response would be within the control of the researcher; and it is within the range of personal, telephone or postal questionnaires that selection is normally made.

3 The correct answer is **a**.

'Demographic' refers to vital statistics concerning the nature of the people in a community — not, for example, their possessions or their hobbies, but elements basically to do with who and what they are. So sex, age and race are demographic features, but income is not normally so regarded.

4 The correct answer is **a**.

Have you ever tried to get a decision made between two or more people? Individual decision making is almost invariably faster than group decision making. Either can be accurrate; groups are expensive to assemble in terms of facilities and the salaries of the members for the time of the meeting. Individual decision making is not cumbersome, while there are situations in which getting groups together can be difficult, as you will know if you have ever been responsible for such an activity. This, by the way, is a good example of a question where, if in doubt and *after* searching your mind for the theory, you can fall back on common-sense (whatever that might be).

5 The correct answer is **b**.

Many a problem has gone unsolved because the person responsible has failed to spot it, especially in personal and interpersonal matters. A good

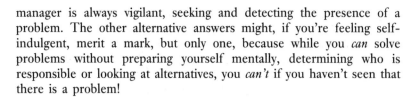

manager is always vigilant, seeking and detecting the presence of a problem. The other alternative answers might, if you're feeling self-indulgent, merit a mark, but only one, because while you *can* solve problems without preparing yourself mentally, determining who is responsible or looking at alternatives, you *can't* if you haven't seen that there is a problem!

6   The correct answer is **d**.

Budgetary control, essential though it is to efficiency, has an air of necessary negative/prevention/control, rather than positive voluntary actions with reward for achievement. It is therefore rarely associated directly with monetary reward.

7   The correct answer is **a**.

The others are purely fictional; although the last may characterize what you do with your brain as the last moments of your examinations approach. .

8   The correct answer is **c**.

The critical path is the longest set of necessary actions. Think about this, because it is only too easy to answer 'the *shortest* inevitable set of actions'. When assembling the egg and chips the critical path follows the peeling of the potatoes, cutting them into chip-shapes, deep-frying them, draining and putting on to plates. This is the *longest* necessary set of actions, each of which must follow the other, cannot be done simultaneously or overlap: frying the eggs, getting the plates, knives and forks out, serving the eggs, locating the salt and pepper, can all be done while the chips are frying.

9   The correct answer is **b**.

Drucker's best known work is the classic *The Practice of Management*, which you may like to dip into as revision, and should certainly read after the exams if you want to be a professional manager.

10   The correct answer is **a**.

But 2 marks also if you said 'all of them'. Planning concerns itself with all forecast future events, and is done systematically by good managers. They range their thoughts and proposals between the short, medium and long term: none is more important than the other and each impinges on the others. Remember also the distinction between forecasting (making suppositions about future situations) and planning (proposing actions to deal with them).

Score 2 marks for each correct answer. What was your score for this topic? Fill it in on the score grid.

If you scored 12 or less and are still a bit shaky on some points go back and look at the study guide again, before proceeding any further.

If you are sure you really understand and are familiar with the topic now, try the 10 further questions which are on pages 171-173.

Alternatively you can go on to the next topic and do all the post-tests together at the end.

Topic 5   Communication

Study guide

This is a sort of compendium chapter of various theories and techniques applied to the general heading of 'communication', or the conveying of effective information from one person or group to another.

Managers spend much of their time engaged in this activity, and the Institute of Bankers examiners rightly concentrate on it, sprinkling the question paper with many opportunities for you to express a studied and systematic understanding of communication in many modes; though beware of seeing, or suggesting, that the solution of communication problems will cure all organizational ills.

The word 'communication' will not necessarily appear in the question, but some of the topic subheadings below might; and you may be expected to discern, detective-like, the examiner's intentions as to answers about communication in case-study answers.

We shall run through this topic under the following heads:

1 'The' model of communication
2 Barriers to communication
3 Communication media in organizations
4 Interpersonal communication skills:
   interviewing
   counselling
   briefing
5 Communication and information technology

Model

In any question specifically on communication it will be of advantage to you to set down the model of communication shown here, because it demonstrates your understanding of the theory. It comes in various forms in different publications, but nobody will disagree with the basic elements in the way a *message* moves, as shown here:

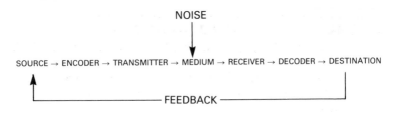

The message *originates* from the Source, who selects the correct *code* and *encodes* it. This means that the person sending the message selects a language — like Written English, or Lower-deck Naval Curses, or Disco Hip, and formulates the message in those terms.

It is then *transmitted* — posted, or shouted, or displayed, via a *medium* (plural: media) like a letter, or voice, or noticeboard, or memo or telephone-call. Here it can be affected by *noise*, meaning anything that can interrupt the message or distort it, such as noise itself, or dislike of the sender by the receiver, or delay.

The message is then *received*, which just means arrives at the place of destination, and has to be *decoded*, that is, the language used must be recognized and translated: this can be problematical — just think of someone who doesn't understand Disco Hip (whatever that might be. . . . .)

If the decoding is successful then the message can be said to have arrived at its *destination*. The sender, however, cannot know that it has been 'received and understood' unless there is *feedback*, a message to confirm those facts.

Learn the model, and then try it out hypothetically, as a revision exercise: first on the message sent to a motorist by a motorcyclist whose parked bike has just been knocked over by the motorist's car.

Then apply it to the Area or Regional Manager having to tell his managers that the bank is demanding detailed extra account statistics on all customers who have house purchase loans.

With these examples fresh in your mind, note that *skills* are needed in all aspects of communication:

— In the selection of *code*, or language: obviously French is no good to a destination person who doesn't speak it; and, less obviously, technical banking language is no good to a customer who doesn't speak it. . .

— In the *transmission*, seeing to it that the message is properly prepared, is sent on time and in the right direction.

— In the selection of *medium* for the most effective conveyance of a particular message (if the building bursts into flame, you don't announce the evacuation by posting a notice on the noticeboard).

— In *receiving*, in having 'Listening' devices present, being open for messages, having an efficient incoming mail room, employing a telephone answering service.

— In *decoding*, recognizing how something is being said, and extracting the real meaning as intended by the sender: being a good listener, being able to overcome accent-prejudice, being able to 'read between the lines'.

— In *feedback*, taking the responsibility of letting the sender know that the message has arrived and is understood.

 Understanding Organisations, p. 356: Handy: Penguin.

Barriers to communication

All of the barriers to effective communication can be lined up against the headings of the model, but it is worth looking at them separately because an exam question is just as likely to be asked about difficulties in communication as about effective communication.

A brief word about *effective*: all business communication should have clear, even explicit, *objectives*, desired end-results in understanding, or resultant attitude change, or action. By effective we shall therefore mean 'achieving the originator's organizational objectives' (how about that — three 'O's — for a probable mark in the exam?).

Barriers prevent communication from being effective: here are some as they appear in the textbooks:

1 Noise itself: the distraction from a properly-sent message because other things are simultaneously attracting the attention of the receiver (like how amazingly attractive the messenger is. . . .)

2 Process or technical problems in the proper functioning of the various physical elements of the model: phone out of order, mail strike, fire in the post room.

3 Semantic (meaning language) problems: the use by the originator of language the destination person or group cannot understand, or can misunderstand, by reason of, say,

> foreign language
> regional accent or dialect
> social class accent or usage

       technical language or jargon
       unfamiliar typeface or writing or symbols
       incorrect semantic level (too difficult!)

4 Psychological barriers: on the part of the source (don't really want you to know, don't think you want to know, am afraid of telling you, will look foolish if I tell you); or on the part of the messenger, the medium; or on the part of the destination person (like to keep myself to myself, don't like to hear bad news, not interested).

5 Wrong medium: see the next section.

6 Wrong channel: message sent to the wrong person, not redirected, lost in transmission.

In a case study answer, should you be asked what has gone wrong with a communication system, *don't* just select the barrier you think is causing the problem: list/outline *all* the possible problems or barriers and then select, judiciously, the one you think is the culprit and outline how the barrier can be surmounted. Remember that you are there to prove to the examiner not just that you can solve problems, but that you have *studied* so as to be able to do so.

Communication media in organizations

Before reading this, think of all the ways people communicate with each other in organizations. If you take a few minutes, your list will probably not differ much from the one given below.

You can easily be asked to discuss the advantages and disadvantages of certain communication methods/media and you may like to bear in mind the *magic three*: three advantages and three disadvantages at least in this kind of answer makes a nicely balanced paper!

Here's a three: *written, oral* and *visual* communication.

Written means written, typed or printed; examples are letters, memo's, cheques, legal documents, handwritten notes, statements, books, handouts, advertising leaflets, articles in magazines and so on.

Oral means spoken (avoid 'verbal', which means 'in words', and although often used as a synonym for oral, which means 'with the mouth', it isn't). Examples at work are briefings, interviews, conversations, presentations, meetings, and conferences.

Visual means in pictures. These appear as posters, house journals, advertising material, illustrations in training, instructional and circular material, and video/television pictures.

Good managers/good communicators make careful choices of media for messages, because putting the right message into the wrong medium loses the effectiveness of the message, which is why the famous communication theorist, Marshall McCluhan, entitled his best known book *The Medium IS the Message* (possible clever exam mark? — depends on clever examiner!).

And now here are three advantages and disadvantages for each method:

	Advantages	Disadvantages
1 Written communication	Permanent Transferable Legally necessary	Slow to produce Cold and impersonal Reactions unseen
2 Oral communication	Immediate Reactions perceived Emotion possible	Impermanent Not always binding Expensive
3 Visual communication	Immediate and fast Dramatic impact Interesting	No lengthiness possible Complexity difficult Unconventional

To revise, get these into your head, working out in a commonsense way what is meant at each point; and try — even if you fail — to add one to every category: this will force you to clarify the thoughts suggested above in your mind. Now look at Topic 9, Section 9.6. It shows certain 'communication patterns'. Try to see which medium fits which of the patterns described.

Interpersonal communication skills

Interviewing

Irrespective of the purpose of an interview (discipline, grievance, customer, appraisal, briefing, counselling etc.), this is an interaction between two people, with certain characteristics which define it and the skills required to conduct it, as follows; learn these five defining characteristics:

— *Objectives*: interviewer and interviewee will both have objectives, things they want to achieve by the end of the interview. A clear statement and a clear view of them, and skills in directing the interview towards them, chracterize the good interviewer.
— *Role* difference between interviewer and interviewee: the interviewer should be in charge (though not dominant or aggressive), so that the interview is efficient, something required by the interviewee too.

— *Formality* is a feature, and expected — useful even; but it can give rise to tension, which should be carefully managed — usually reduced, but not invariably — by the skilled interviewer.

— *Structure* is needed, at least in the form of beginning/opening, middle/body, and end/close; and this requires careful *planning* by the expert interviewer, especially of the next characteristic.

— *Investigation*, or questioning: the essence of interviews, because if there is nothing to be discovered, if all is known, the interview is not an interview, but probably a speech. Investigation requires skills-development, probably via training.

Counselling

An entire book in itself! It will have to suffice to say that the good manager, in engaging in counselling:

— *Discerns need* in a member of staff for career or personal development, or problem-solution counsel.

— *Ensures privacy* for the counselling session.

— *Encourages expression* by the staff member about subject of counsel.

— *Avoids direct advice* except when specifically requested, and not always even then.

— *Encourages development of own solutions*, courses of action, alternatives, by staff member, relating them to formal or informal objectives.

— *Supports selected action*, suggests means of implementation, offers resources, help and support.

— *Monitors* career, personal development or problem-solution.

Briefing

Briefing is one of the central tasks of the manager in a decisional or leadership or developmental situation, but it is usually poorly executed because it's not necessarily seen as a communication task-skill, more often as a talent (that statement alone could net you a point).

Once again, breaking it up into its constituent definitional characteristics indicates what personal skills are needed to be effective in, and will help you revise for a possible question on, briefing:

— *Grasps own brief*, understanding all the detail and minutiae of the matter to be brief.

— *Sets objectives* in terms of understanding and feedback from the briefed team.

— *Selects team* to be briefed on need-to-know basis.

— *Plans briefing session*, composing, structuring and writing briefing notes.
— *Assembles material* such as briefing or handout notes, illustrations or brochures, in advance of session.
— *Gives briefing* in understandable terms, with motivation/exhortation elements to ensure cooperation.
— *Encourages feedback* for complete understanding among team.
— *Requires read-back* ('Tell me what I've briefed you to do) to check and confirm that understanding.
— *Initiates action*: first steps reminded and encouraged.
— *Monitors progress* of briefed project, adjusting and adding amended running briefings to keep on course.

Communications and information technology

It is important for aspiring managers to be knowledgeable about the possibilities offered by information technology, and the examiners would wish you to demonstrate that you are aware of them. You need once again to be systematic about how you express yourself in an exam question: here is one way.

1 Individual work

Wordprocessors freely available means faster, more accurate, more easily edited, altered, stored and retrieved documentation.
Electronic diaries in the form of large-storage hand-computers make executives more efficient.
Desk terminals keep the manager up to date, present information efficiently, allow rapid calculation and data manipulation.

2 Person to person

Desk telephone technology improving; personal/desk 'exchange'-type hand sets with memories, re-dialling facilities.
Portable telephone network systems for use anywhere.
Radiopaging to contact people away from the office.

3 Person to group

Photocopying in colour, faster, with better cut-paste and collation features improves the dissemination of documentation.
Video tape recording allows messages to be conveyed to audience by persons not present.
Closed circuit TV allows personal contact at remote premises.
Conference telephones, some with visual circuitry, allow meetings between people at a distance.

4 Office to office

Mainframe computers with multiple distant terminals are carrying more and more information (perhaps you've noticed in the branch!).

Telex systems are faster, quieter, more widespread than ever.

Wordprocessor links and networks are now possible over telephone landlines: you type on yours, the words appear on mine.

Facsimile machines for transmitting pictures are now very sophisticated.

This is just one way of being systematic in your answers on this — or any — topic. Memorize lists, and in revision, add to them or adjust them for your own understanding. Make those lists the structure of your exam answer, relevantly and economically. Let the examiner know that you have studied and can reproduce information, and then can judiciously select from that information to answer your questions.

Once you feel confident about your knowledge of this topic, try to answer the 10 multiple choice questions which follow.

Multiple choice questions

1 Which of the following does not normally appear in the traditional model of communication:

   a   aerial?
   b   transmitter?
   c   receiver?
   d   source?

answer

2 Between which of the following points does noise usually appear:

   a   source and transmitter?
   b   transmitter and receiver?
   c   receiver and decoder?
   d   decoder and destination?

answer

3 One of the following classifications of communication includes two of the others:

   a   written communication.
   b   oral communication.
   c   verbal communication.
   d   visual communication.

answer

4 Which of these would be described as a process problem in communication:

   a   having run out of envelopes?
   b   not speaking the language?
   c   going blind with rage at the sender?
   d   stopping listening because you're bored?

answer

5 To be effective, an interview needs to be:

    a planned.
    b early in the day.
    c by the immediate superior.
    d short.

6 To be effective, an interview does not have to have:

    a structure.
    b objectives.
    c privacy.
    d assertiveness.

7 To brief effectively, the manager *need* not include in preparation:

    a grasping own brief.
    b hiring outside facilities for the briefing session.
    c preparing own contribution.
    d assembling all relevant documentation.

8 One of the following is not necessary during the briefing session:

    a monitoring the reactions of the audience.
    b maintaining a reasonable pace.
    c insisting on silence throughout the formal part.
    d clarifying first steps in the action required.

9 A good counsellor *always*:

    a prepares a schedule of advice before the counselling session.
    b gives advice gradually, cumulatively, during the session.
    c waits until the end of the session, then invariably gives advice.

d supports with advice the decisions of the counselled.

 answer

10 A facsimile device:

    a is just like a photocopier, but only reproduces pictorial material.
    b sends pictorial material from one location to another.
    c produces 'identikit'-style computerized portraits.
    d is a computer that types out speech-input from a microphone.

 _answer_

Answers follow on pages 92-94. Score 2 marks for each correct answer.

Answers

1 The correct answer is **a**.

While the radioelectronic analogy is used throughout the traditional model, aerials do not appear. After all, the use of a radio or TV aerial would imply only those media, whereas the model is intended to apply to all communication media.

2 The correct answer is **b**.

Notice that the question asked 'usually . . . . . .', because noise *can* appear anywhere, since it is anything which can distract attention from the clear passage of the message. Look again at the entire model, and with an example in mind, such as those required as a revision exercise in the study guide, think about things which could constitute noise at all other points than between transmitter and receiver, although this is still the stretch where noise is most likely to disturb the message. You can only allow yourself the consolationary half-a-mark if you said, instead of **b**, 'all of them'.

3 The correct answer is **c**.

A common mistake, found in even some textbooks, is to suggest that 'oral' is the same as 'verbal'. Colloquially it really does not matter, but technically it does (dentists don't give you a verbal examination, nor do you get one at 'O'-level French); and technically 'oral' means 'with the mouth'; 'verbal' means 'in words'. Verbal therefore includes 'written' as well as 'oral' — but look at the wording of your disciplinary procedure, where I'll bet it starts with an informal 'verbal' warning whereas to be precise it means 'oral'.

4 The correct answer is **a**.

A process problem is exactly that: a problem in the physical process, which running out of envelopes would constitute. Not speaking the language is a semantic problem, and getting cross or bored are psychological problems.

5 The correct answer is **a**.

Interviews should always be planned, even if the interviewee demands to be seen immediately. Even the most important customer will wait five minutes and define that as 'immediately', while you sort out the file and gather information and plan the questions you need to ask.

While each of the other alternative answers may apply to certain interviews, they are not universal recipes for sensible conduct, as planning is.

6 The correct answer is **d**.

Interviews must be structured, if only in terms of having a controlled opening, an investigatory or information-exchanging middle, and a firm and clear end. No managerially sound interview can proceed efficiently without clear objectives in the mind of at least one of the participants, preferably the interviewer's, and even more preferably, both parties. In most kinds of interview, such as grievance, or discipline, or customer, or appraisal, or counselling, privacy is important. Assertiveness is not at all necessary as a characteristic of the effective interview, although it is important that the interviewer remains in control of the proceedings so as to move in the direction of the objectives.

7 The correct answer is **b**.

Fairly obvious, really, although outside facilities sometimes enhance the importance of the subject of the briefing.

8 The correct answer is **c**.

However, insisting on silence is common, and traditionally some more old-fashioned managers believe in a classroom attitude to the brief, though one may suspect that it is because they are afraid of aggressive comments or questions they can't answer; or if the argument of the briefing is very complex, it may be better to keep questions or comments to the end. But if the aim is understanding, then permitting clarification during the course of the briefing session is almost invariably more effective. Monitoring audience reaction so as to adjust to it, maintaining pace to avoid boredom, and clarifying the first steps, are necessary to effective briefing.

9 The correct answer is **d**.

Counselling is *not* advice-giving. It is essentially active listening, followed by encouragement to the subject to pursue courses of action on which they have, with help, decided themselves. The counsellor can provide suggestions as to a range of alternatives, and can help in prognosticating the outcomes to certain courses of action, and can advise on the implementation of the chosen course. In view of this, you might consider yourself unfairly treated if you said **a**, 'preparing a schedule of advice': but the only true answer is **d**.

10 The correct answer is **b**.

No such device as one which only reproduces pictures; there are devices for the build up of pictures from library materials, available pretty freely for any personal computer; the speech-translator is invented but not yet commercially available, although one can buy computer programs that respond to simple oral (not verbal, note. . . . . . .) commands; but a facsimile device is in many ways similar to Telex except that it sends/receives pictorial messages, with an almost total accuracy over literally any distance on earth.

Score 2 marks for each correct answer. What was your score for this topic? Fill it in on the score grid.

If you scored 12 or less and are still a bit shaky on some points go back and look at the study guide again, before proceeding any further.

If you are sure you really understand and are familiar with the topic now, try the 10 further questions which are on pages 173-175.

Alternatively you can go on to the next topic and do all the post-tests together at the end.

Topic 6   Leadership and Management Styles

Study guide

This is another subject in which what you know will be useable in case-study type questions. It is also one in which 'models' abound, and therefore examination point-scoring is possible if you have memorized the model, diagram or list involved.

Take care to distinguish between 'management' and 'leadership': the former is all those activities covered by this syllabus, and the latter has to do with personal activities influencing the behaviour of subordinates. However, 'management style' normally refers to approaches to subordinates above all, but with some added element of how that is related to production, as we will see. In this chapter, it is suggested that you revise Leadership and Management Style together, and they will be dealt with as follows:

1 Leadership:
   Traits
   Situations
   Contingency
   Action centred leadership
2 Management style:
   One-dimension: Tannenbaum & Schmidt
   Two-dimension: Blake & Mouton
   Three-dimension: Reddin

Leadership

If there is a case study question where you know that what the examiner wants is for you to discuss leadership, remember to cite your leadership model(s) and then apply the principles to the case. You may start by dismissing traits or qualities, as most textbooks do these days. . .

Traits

Ask a manager what qualities a leader needs and you'll get a list. Now ask another manager and you'll get a different list, or perhaps one with the same words but different order or meaning. Even if they agreed, if they then apply those traits to leaders such as Ghenghis Khan or Alexander the Great or Winston Churchill, they would find they don't all necessarily apply; or there are those you know who have the traits in some measure, but couldn't lead a bunch of thirsty bankers to the pub.

And what use is all this to you, you ask? Well, it is in fact useful to note the above because *it is currently out of fashion to think about leadership in terms of traits and qualities.* By all means state a few leadership qualities, but then score points by saying that 'some great leaders lack some of them, and some who have all are not good leaders'.

In summary, nowadays it is better to think of leadership as something that you *do* rather than a leader being something that you *are*.

Situational leadership

The buzz-name is Mary Parker Follett, and the situational leadership theory is that the best leader is the one best suited to a particular situation, with the knowledge or expertise to handle that, if not all situations. The Celts and the Sioux Indians, for example, used to select War Chiefs for the sole purpose of leading the tribe in battle, and *not* continuing as leader in peace-time.

In management, this would mean leadership passing from one team member to another as the task altered; seems sensible, but hardly practical in the standard banking set-up. It is more applicable to the sort of flexibly structured trouble-shooting team you might find (or rather expect to find) dealing with special projects or major organizational changes, such as mergers.

Contingency

A certain E. Fiedler developed, from his research, a theory called the contingency theory of leadership effectiveness, effectiveness depending on:

1 How well the leader gets on with subordinates
2 How structured the task is
3 The leader's organizational power to punish or reward

Briefly, Fiedler note that managers were either task-oriented or relationship-oriented (more of this later), and that task-oriented leaders were more effective when the situation was *either* very favourable or very unfavourable to them in terms of the above three factors; relationship-oriented managers were effective when the factors were neither favourable nor unfavourable. Or put another way,

	Very favourable or very unfavourable	Not particularly favourable or unfavourable
Task-oriented	Effective	Ineffective
Relationship-oriented	Ineffective	Effective

Action-centred leadership

John Adair is the name to remember, and he said that you must start from this basic position:

1 What a leader leads is a group
2 A group has sets of group needs
3 A good leader does things to satisfy those needs

So you must know what the sets of group needs are, and take actions to satisfy them — action-centred leadership. In fact, says Adair, groups have three sets of needs, namely,

Task needs, to get the tasks done, well, and indeed competitively well;
Group maintenance, or team needs, to maintain cohesion, spirit and morale;
Individual needs, those of each member of the group (when revising, check out Maslow, Topic 7).

Adair's model is *always* drawn as follows: exam Brownie points for reproducing the familiar overlapping circles:

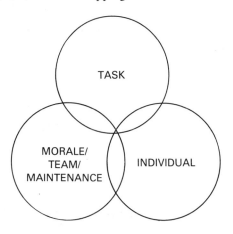

They overlap because any shortcoming in one affects another, and where one is being satisfied, that contributes to another. Thus if team/morale needs are not being satisfied, the task is not completed as

well as if they were; and if an individual's needs are satisfied, that will contribute to group morale.

> Here is one example of *observable actions* that leaders can take to satisfy each of the above needs: for revision, think of *two more* in each category:
>
> *Task*: Sets manageable targets and makes them known
> *Team*: Makes a point of congratulating good team performance
> *Individual*: Gives people tasks that recognize special talents

> *Understanding Orrganisations*, p. 96: Handy: Penguin.
> *Organisational Behaviour*, p. 377: Buchanan and Huczynski: Prentice Hall.

Management style

Frankly, should you choose to, you could also use any of the above models to apply to a case study, outlining the principles — and drawing the diagram — and then using the points to apply to the case. However, if the question refers to management style as such, then the examiner will be expecting *at least* the first two of the following models.

The style continuum

More than one author has suggested that there is a continuous spectrum of leadership styles, but they frequently suggest four points along that continuum. Memorize *Tannenbaum and Schmidt*, and *Rensis Likert*, as names associated with these four, and memorize the four styles:

Autocratic	Benevolent autocratic	Consultative	Participative
Manager tells, punishes if disobedience; makes all decisions	Manager tells, punishes but for own good; looks after staff	Manager consults staff, takes into account; makes own decisions	Group makes decisions; manager implements decisions

Where they referred to the style adopted by the managers of an entire organization, these were called System 1, 2, 3 and 4 by Likert. The only problem is that the second seems to get a different name in every different textbook (Paternalistic, Persuasive, Missionary, Selling. . . .). Likert's research in the USA indicated a correlation between the business success of companies and System 4, Participative Management;

Ashridge (score a point) Management College found the Consultative style more successful in the UK. This model is highly applicable in case study questions — sorry to nag, but *state it* and *apply it*.

Blake and Mouton's grid

These consultants, acknowledging the continuum of styles, pointed out that concern for people was not enough to describe managerial style; the concern for production also had to be accounted for, and they did this in a second dimension: *learn* and *reproduce* this diagram, *accurately* in the examination wherever the concept of management style is appropriate:

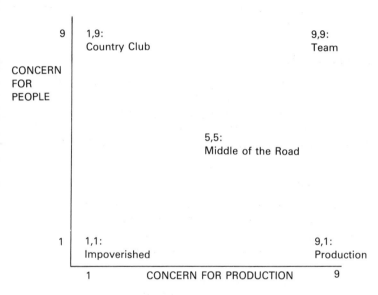

It is not for us to discuss this here; but as a revision exercise, think about the management style of managers at each corner and in the middle, with their high or low concern for staff or for output. In an answer, reproduce the diagram and describe (a) the actual style of the appropriate character, and (b) the more appropriate style.

Reddin's 3D

W.J. Reddin added a third dimension, effectiveness, (E), by which he really meant appropriateness. Calling 'concern for production' 'task orientation' (TO) and 'concern for people' 'relationship orientation' (RO), his diagram looked like this, with his nicknames for extreme styles included:

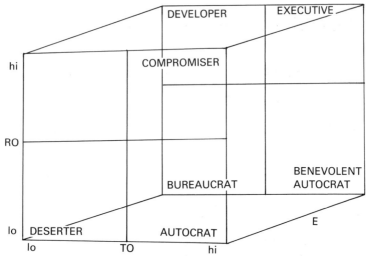

Again, as a revision exercise, think about high and low task orientation, production orientation and effectiveness/appropriateness for each one of these eight in turn, and consider the appropriateness of the style description. An example to start you off:

> The *Bureaucrat* is not concerned for getting production out, nor is he interested in whether people like his decisions or not. But if he's *paid to be like that*, that is, that those orientations are appropriate/effective to the job he holds, then Bureaucrat is a good name for him. If he's like that, and he's *not* supposed to be like that, then Deserter is a better name.

Now you try it for the other seven. This being more complex, if you can get it right and reproduce it appropriately it would certainly do you no harm in the examinations.

At the end of this topic, to remind you: rarely a direct question on leadership or management style, but whether there is or if the topic comes up in a case study, set out the principles in the form of a list or preferably the diagrams as shown above or in your textbooks; then apply them to the case or with suggested examples to prove you know and *have studied* your stuff.

Once you feel confident about your knowledge of this topic, try to answer the 10 multiple choice questions which follow.

Multiple choice questions

1 Which of the following are not group needs according to Adair:

a task needs?
b group maintenance needs?
c organizational needs?
d individual needs?

answer

2 Of the following, which is wrongly described:

a 9,1: task-oriented management?
b 9,9: uncommitted management?
c 5,5: middle of the road management?
d 1,9: country club management?

answer

3 Select the phrase which best describes Consultative management style:

a manager consults staff but usually takes no notice.
b manager consults staff and always goes along with suggestions.
c manager consults staff and always agrees with some of them.
d manager consults staff and takes views into consideration.

answer

4 Select the phrase which best describes Participative style:

a decisions are made by the manager with the help of the group.
b the group makes the decisions, the manager gets them implemented.
c decisions are made by the group with the help of the manager.
d part of the decisions are made by the group, part by manager.

answer

5 In Fiedler's theory of effective leadership, which of these does effective leadership not necessarily depend on:

 a the relationship between the manager and his subordinates?
 b the structure of the task?
 c the leader's power of punishment and reward?
 d how intraverted or extraverted the manager is?

6 What does 'effectiveness' mean in Reddin's 3D theory:

 a having effective orientations for the job being done?
 b the ability to produce high output?
 c getting people to work effectively?
 d consistently being able to put plans into effect?

7 In action-centred leadership, why do task needs and team needs intersect:

 a because getting the job done raises morale?
 b because backlogs lower morale and affect teamwork?
 c because low morale adversely affects task performance?
 d because high morale contributes to effective working?

8 Why are leadership theories based on qualities difficult to accept:

 a because no reputable theorist has put one forward?
 b because there is little agreement on a list of qualities?
 c because other theories appeal more to good leaders?
 d because no theory helps people to be better leaders?

9 Which of the following describes the Developer:

 a high RO, low TO, high E?
 b low RO, high TO, high E?

c high TO, high RO, low E?
d low TO, high RO, low E?

 answer

10 Situational leadership is, most closely:

a getting the right leader properly selected.
b developing as a good leader because you've been selected.
c being a good leader in certain situations and not others.
d selecting the leader by appropriate skills, task by task.

 _answer_

Answers follow on pages 104-106. Score 2 marks for each correct answer.

Answers

1 The correct answer is **c**.

Adair's is the simple and familiar model of action centred leadership and you must be very familiar with it. I am inclined to suggest that if you got this answer wrong you should *deduct* a mark!

2 The correct answer is **b**.

Jot down the diagram, or refer to it in the study guide, or even think about it in mathematical terms, and you'll see that 9,9 must imply high on both axes, Concern for Production and Concern for People. This cannot mean uncommitted; quite the reverse, in fact, and 9,9 is the ideal for which Blake and Mouton suggest managers should aim, and which they refer to as Team Management. Note that the scales do not go from 0 but from 1, since *no* concern for either of the axial elements is not a possible stance, only a *minimum* concern.

3 The correct answer is **d**.

Consulting and ignoring is not a consultative style, and is soon spotted by the staff, who will cease to make suggestions after a while. Consulting and always complying implies weak management if the actual power to decide is supposed to be, and is culturally accepted to be, with the manager, or is truly participative. Agreeing with some but not all the staff is hardly a describeable general style, even if there are some managers who behave in that way. Consultative means consults staff, takes views into consideration, and with that and other data, makes managerial decisions.

4 The correct answer is **b**.

The participative style, dependent on the organization accepting it as reasonable behaviour for its managers, means that the managers actually see their role as implementers of decisions made exclusively by the group with the managers as members. So answer **c** could merit half-a-mark, but it isn't the closest definition because it does not indicate that which distinguishes the manager, which is the element of implementation.

5 The correct answer is **d**.

It is by no means the character of the manager which plays a part in

Fiedler's theory, but mainly power and relationships.

6 The correct answer is **a**.

Colloquially, the rest are all excellent definitions of effectiveness for managers in the field. However, Reddin uses the word in a very particular manner, to indicate a relationship between managers' inclinations or orientations towards people and tasks, and whether those inclinations/orientations are *appropriate*, or 'effective' to the task–people mix. Thus there are jobs where high orientation towards people is ineffective (such as singlehandedly supervising the junction of an oil pipeline in Alaska), and some where it is essential (such as missionary to the Eskimos whose land the pipeline crosses). Just remember the strong connection between *effective* and *appropriate*.

7 The correct answer is **all of them**.

Draw the diagram — three overlapping circles labelled Task, Team and Individual. Then observe that all the answers refer to the overlap between tasks getting done and team morale: **a** from positive Task to positive Team; **b** from negative Task to negative Team; **c** from negative Team to negative Task; and **d** from positive Team to positive Task. You can do this for all the overlaps, and you may like to try it, because it is almost the whole point of Adair having designed the diagram in that way.

8 The correct answer is **b**.

It could be accepted that all are true to an extent, and a grudging mark for that answer (though none for selecting any single one but **b**). Please beware of suggesting your own list of preferred qualities. It cuts no ice whatsoever with the examiners, and unless you have a PhD in social science or are Chief Executive of your bank they have no good reason to accept it. Should you have found a good list in the writings of a reputable theorist, then reproduce it with a reference to the author, by all means.

9 The correct answer is **a**.

You should have spotted the terms used by Reddin in the 3D theory, set forth in his book entitled *Managerial Effectiveness*, and you should be able to name and place each of the eight extreme points of the box. The Developer style is as set out in **a**; **b** refers to Benevolent Autocrat; **c** describes the Compromiser style, and **d** the Missionary style of management. An additional point worth noting about Reddin is that he introduced the notion of Style Flex (flexibility): the good manager may have a dominant style, but can change and adapt to the present circumstances.

10 The correct answer is **d**.

The others are important: the proper selection of the right leader can make an enormous difference to a group; people do develop as leaders just from being put into leadership situations; some people are good leaders in some types of situation and not others, and this should be accounted for. But the question refers to situational leadership, a clue to Mary Parker Follett which you should have spotted, and **d** is closest to her definition.

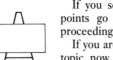

Score 2 marks for each correct answer. What was your score for this topic? Fill it in on the score grid.

If you scored 12 or less and are still a bit shaky on some points go back and look at the study guide again, before proceeding any further.

If you are sure you really understand and are familiar with the topic now, try the 10 further questions which are on pages 176-178.

Alternatively you can go on to the next topic and do all the post-tests together at the end.

Topic 7   Motivation

Study guide

One way or another, there is always a question on motivation *or* you should be able to incorporate the material in this chapter into one of your answers. Sometimes it's disguised in a case-study type question; but there is no management without people, and people don't work without motivation. By the way, it is in this topic that the great fallacy that you can pass without study is most prevalent — and truly false. Whatever their own views or developed knowledge may be, the examiners have in their minds some famous, precise and established models of human motivation, and will expect to *recognize* them in what you produce in your paper, because they know how you have been, or should have been, taught. There follows an account of some of the main models; but since wages and salaries still form a basic part of motivation systems, there is also a section on this topic at the end. The shape of the chapter is, then, as shown in the diagram.

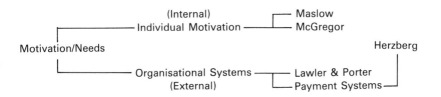

The reason for this is that motivation can mean 'What drives me to do anything, from within myself?', or it can mean, 'How is the organization I work for set up to motivate me?'. The *names* of the people mentioned in the diagram are *vital*: you must know what they said and how they spell their names, which you must mention to prove you know your stuff.

Motivation

Motivation is closely related to needs. The 'distance' between where I am and where I want to be can be defined by the word 'need': the greater the distance, the greater the need; and if I am where I want to be, no distance = no needs. Motivation is the *drive to satisfy needs*. Please note that the drive may not be sufficient to move me to actually do anything: I could do with a cup of coffee as I write this, but I'm continuing to type, because the need to finish this chapter is currently greater and is moving me to action.

Man's needs are in fact multiple and complex, a fact discovered in the management sense by Mayo during the Hawthorne Experiments (see Topic 1): people worked better under certain social conditions than under others. To be able to answer questions on motivation, therefore, you must know what the central theorists said about people's needs, and the way the organizations they work for set themselves up so that people can satisfy their needs at work, for the benefit of the organization (a very carefully-worded sentence: read it again).

Individual motivation (internal)

Maslow

The central model of motivation in Western civilised man is that of Abraham Maslow. If you're not familiar with this you can't pass a question on motivation.

Maslow suggested that man's needs form a hierarchy, from the basic at the bottom to the subtle/complex at the top. People need company, food, artistic satisfaction, security and other things, but they don't arise at random, or with equal degrees of urgency. According to Maslow, the order is as follows, with the more powerful at the bottom:

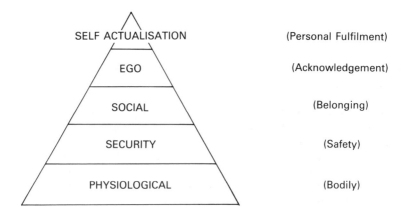

SELF ACTUALISATION	(Personal Fulfilment)
EGO	(Acknowledgement)
SOCIAL	(Belonging)
SECURITY	(Safety)
PHYSIOLOGICAL	(Bodily)

Always draw the diagram with its triangle, using the words on the left. Having all the needs, I'd first want to satisfy the Bodily needs (hunger, thirst, fatigue), then I'd wish to secure my lines to the next meal, and be Safe. Only then would I seek the company and liking of others; and having done that, I'd want people to recognize and acknowledge the value of me as an individual (ego means 'I' in Latin); and finally I'd ask myself, what potential is there in me that I want to fulfil? Note that if I am starving to death that last question does not occur to me, at least not at the time.

The triangular diagram is one set of buzz-words you must use to prove to the examiner that you know Maslow. Some others are 'A need, once satisfied, is no longer a need': if you're hungry and you eat you're no longer hungry. And the word 'prepotent' or 'prepotency': once a lower need is satisfied, the next one above becomes prepotent — comes into action. Finally, and vitally, the whole theory is called 'Maslow's Hierarchy of Needs'.

Please do not think, if we treat it lightly here, that this theory is unimportant. If you have time, check it out in any textbook about management and motivation.

Prepare carefully in your mind — or better still in jotted notes — ways in which you or others like you could satisfy each one of the needs delineated at work. This will be an invaluable exercise, since the exam question is never pure, always applied when it comes to motivation. So do that *now*!

Organisational Behaviour, p. 52: Buchanan and Huczynski: Prentice Hall.

McGregor

Douglas McGregor wrote a great deal, but he only ever said *one* thing which will help you pass this exam. It was as follows:

> Some managers hold the belief that human beings respond only to punishment and reward, and if you don't do anything to them, they remain motionless. This is called Theory X. Some managers believe that human beings are naturally self-motivated, and if you don't do anything to them, they will fizz about finding constructive things to do. This is called Theory Y. Human beings will in fact respond better to the latter managers than to the former.

And that's it. Please note that it is not relevant whether Theory X or

Theory Y is *true*, and in fact there are some of whom X is true, some of whom Y is true, and most of whom both are true under one set of circumstances or another. The important thing for McGregor is that if your boss expects you to be idle and makes that clear in word and deed, you are less likely to go out of your way to work well than if that boss starts from the premise that you are a willing and cooperative person. So you can speak of Theory X managers and Theory Y managers, but not correctly of Theory X or Theory Y staff.

Organizational systems (external)

Lawler and Porter

Sometimes referred to as 'expectancy theory' (a useful in-group phrase), Lawler and Porter showed what influences there were on the relationship between motivation and performance, which had largely to do with what people expect out of life. *This too is a model the examiners expect to see*, and for you to demonstrate your knowledge you must show that you are thoroughly familiar with it.

Every textbook you pick up has a different diagram to show what Lawler & Porter said: but most of them look a bit like this, and if you reproduce it, you'll get your marks:

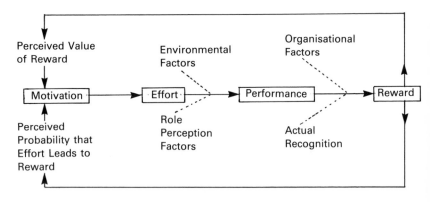

What this diagram tells us (and the examiner) is that just because I'm motivated does not mean that I will perform well against organizational standards, but that there are factors which interpose. Most importantly, *motivation* leads to *effort*, and this leads to *performance* only if

a   my ability is sufficient and I see the work as part of my job — 'role perception factors' on the diagram; and b 'environmental factors' such as the economic climate, or available materials, or the competition, permit my efforts to be translated into performance.

It also suggests that there are factors which get between *performance* and *reward* — familiar to us all — like whether there even exist methods for rewarding the performance, such as incentive schemes or bonuses ('organizational factors'); and of course there is performance that goes unrewarded because the boss doesn't notice it or ascribe it correctly ('actual recognition').

Very important, and the central pillar of the L&P argument, are the two factors between *reward* and *motivation* on the feedback loop:

a Perceived value of reward: it's no use offering you a can of fishing worms, of whatever guaranteed effectiveness, as a reward unless you fish: unless the reward is of value to *you*, it isn't going to feed back into your motivation towards fresh effort.

b Perceived probability that effort will lead to reward: it's also no use offering you something you do not believe I will or can deliver — that would probably be actually demotivating, such as if I promise you promotion for performance when you *know* that it's really based on length of service.

It is these two factors which give the name 'expectancy theory' to this depiction of the relationships betwen motivation, effort, performance and reward: my motivation depends on what I expect to get out of it.

Vroom

Victor Vroom, also an Expectancy theorist, suggested a simple formula: that the level of motivation in the staff was a direct *function* of the perceived probability that effort would lead to reward and the perceived value of the reward. The former he called 'expectancy' and the latter 'valency'. The formula, therefore, reads:

Level of Motivation = Expectancy × Valency

He also suggests methods of putting a calculable value to these variables, but you do not need to study these for your examinations. Just grasp the concept and be able to reproduce and explain the formula.

Payment systems

No theorist discounts the power of payment in motivation; but they can tend to either take it for granted, or relegate it to unimportance, or assume you have enough of it to want to concentrate on other factors.

But payment is important, and you must understand what is contained in what is known as 'reward packages' — quantifiable rewards for work.

Do note that this section of this chapter could have been included under Topic 8, 'Personnel Practices': but to be realistic, rewards are motivating. Should a non-motivation question come up concerning payment systems, however, don't forget to use the information below to answer it!

 Essentially, and concentrating here on what you probably get if you work for a bank, there are not just salaries but also other built-in benefits. It is worth learning a list like this off by heart:

Holidays	Bonuses and share options
Pensions	Cheap/free leisure facilities
Advantageous loans	Medical insurance (at specified levels)
Productivity schemes	Company car (at specified levels,

— and add to it such other measureable benefits you get, or others get in outside businesses, for your revision purposes (like cheap or free company product, suggestion-scheme bonuses, long-service awards, company car/expenses, clothing allowances, school fees, holiday subsidies etc.).

The basic reward is the wage or salary, and basic to that is fairness. There are a number of possible systems to ensure that wage payment systems are fair, and different textbooks will give different selections of ways of ensuring fair payment. There will be two elements common to these selections:

1 You have to get the different jobs aligned so that there is equal payment for equal work, and extra payment for work more important to the organization.

2 You then have to ensure that, at every level, the monetary and other rewards compare in your organization with what is being offered outside it.

There are *factor systems*, which analyse and list the factors in jobs such as personality, skills, experience, responsibilities.

There are *classification systems* where jobs are grouped and compared under headings and yours can be fitted in to one or another heading.

There are *ranking systems* where jobs are rank-ordered in comparison with each other, according to complexity or importance to the organization.

And there are (or more importantly for you there *is*) specialized systems which can be a combination of the above, such as the HAY/MSL system used by the UK clearing banks.

This set up a number of bench-mark jobs such as filing clerk, cashier, senior clerk, and so on, based on a points system for elements of job-content like complexity, experience needed and responsibility for possible loss to the bank; it then set four clerical grades (1–4) and the banks lined up all the clerical jobs into those grades.

Then for each grade a band of remuneration was suggested, with a minimum, a target and a maximum salary. This is so that one may recognize extra effort or talent or service in one grade without needing to promote to another grade to give better monetary reward.

This can be illustrated with a diagram, which incidentally shows why a Grade 2 can in some circumstances be a better paid job than a Grade 3:

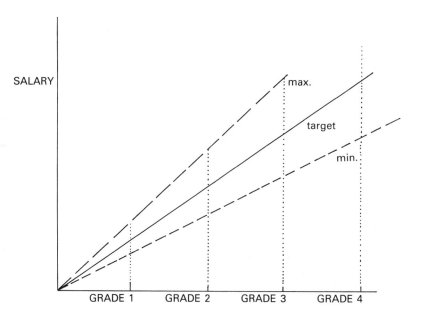

It is *essential* to note that it is *jobs* which are graded, not the incumbent: you are not a grade 2 — you occupy a grade 2 job. More will be found about this in Topic 8.

HAY/MSL also evaluated the minimum manager's salary. All other salaries are agreed separately by the banks, pro-rata, and until recently in agreement with each other; but in the late 1980s there are clear signs of each bank making more and more local agreements on all sorts of matters, including remuneration: it does you no harm to give examples of this where appropriate, from your own experience or knowledge of your own or other banks.

Herzberg

Fred Herzberg's (approximately) mid-1950s 'theory' arose out of some research he did into the attitudes towards job-satisfaction among American working people. In it he asked two questions which at the time he could not have realized were so significantly different. In essence they were, 'What was it that gave you the most satisfaction at work in the last year?', and 'What gave you the most dissatisfaction?'.

What might have been expected was a continuum of answers, such that one factor if present gave satisfaction, and if absent dissatisfaction. **This distinctly did not happen: the factors which gave satisfaction were different ones from those which gave satisfaction.**

Calling the satisfiers 'motivators' and the dissatisfiers 'Hygiene Factors' — *learn these* — Herzberg noted that motivators had to do with the job itself, and dissatisfiers with its circumstances or environment. Most importantly,

Hygiene factors, if poor or absent, give rise to dissatisfaction but if good or present give little positive satisfaction, if any.
Best typical example — working conditions: you don't go to work looking forward to the floral decorations; but the smell of the rotting floorboads could persuade you to stay in bed.

Motivators, if poor or absent, give little positive dissatisfaction, but if good or present give satisfaction.
Best typical example — sense of achievement: knowing there won't be any today is a little depressing, if not constantly overwhelming; but knowing that today is the day we hit the target may impel you in the direction of the office.

A more complete list (and this list *accurately* reproduced as below will get you marks because it shows you 'know Herzberg') is as follows:

Hygiene factors (dissatisfiers)	Motivators (satisfiers)
Work conditions	Achievement
Company policy	Recognition
Supervisor relationships	The work itself
Colleague relationships	Responsibility
Salary (think about it. . .)	Advancement

The point of all this is that if management can identify whether any of these need attention, and accurately pinpoint which ones, they can avoid wasting time and resources. It's no good building a new club cricket pavilion if what is bugging the staff is a lack of promotion opportunities; and it's no good setting up target-hitting bonus schemes if it's the blocked drains which are causing the grumbles.

Many advanced textbooks quote research to show opposite or, a least, different findings from Maslow, McGregor and Herzberg. Both as potential managers and as examination candidates, you may find it instructive or amusing to note that when Herzberg is told this he will tell you why he has a lucky horseshoe hanging in his office even though he doesn't believe in that sort of thing: it's because, he says, 'It works, whether I believe in it or not. . .'.

Once you feel confident about your knowledge of this topic, try to answer the 10 multiple choice questions which follow.

Multiple choice questions

1 Motivation = Valency × Expectancy. This is known as:

   a valency theory.
   b motivation theory.
   c expectancy theory.
   d Maslow's hierarchy.

answer

2 Which of the following said that a need, once satisfied, no longer acts as a need:

   a Maslow?
   b McGregor?
   c Herzberg?
   d Lawler & Porter?

answer

3 Which of the following is a hygiene factor, according to Herzberg:

   a a sense of achievement?
   b company rules and policy?
   c the intricacies of the job itself?
   d responsibility?

answer

4 Social or affiliation needs are:

   a the need to feel that you belong to something.
   b an organization's need to keep its staff happy.
   c the need to have a social life outside work.
   d the need to see lots of people every day.

answer

5   Which of the following most closely describes Theory Y:

    a   man is naturally inert?
    b   man is naturally artistic?
    c   man is naturally rebellious?
    d   man is naturally energetic?

answer

6   Job enrichment is:

    a   giving the staff a rise.
    b   adding extra tasks to prevent boredom.
    c   making jobs more responsible.
    d   letting people know how important they are.

answer

7   Basic salaries in the UK clearing banks are based on:

    a   length of service.
    b   number of accounts at the branch.
    c   job evaluation.
    d   industrial action by staff.

answer

8   According to Lawler and Porter, motivation gives rise most immediately to:

    a   effort.
    b   performance.
    c   reward.
    d   expectancy.

answer

9   Which of these is true of the UK clearing bank's salary system:

    a   there are no fringe benefits?
    b   no Grade 1 can be paid more than a Grade 2?
    c   to get more money you always have to be promoted?

d you can be demoted and still earn the same wages?

10 Motivation can be defined as:

    a paying people to work.
    b the drive to satisfy needs.
    c seeing to it that staff are always happy.
    d getting people to respect you.

 Answers follow on pages 119-121. Score 2 marks for each correct answer.

Answers

1 The correct answer is **c**.

It is the shortest expression of expectancy theory, valency meaning the value that an employee sets on a reward, and expectancy meaning the probability with which that employee believes that effort will produce the reward. Thus, no motivation if either no value to reward, or no probability you'll get it, or both; low motivation if the value of the reward is low, and even lower if it isn't really expected anyway. Motivation will be higher if either the value or the probability of the reward is raised; and motivation at the maximum where there is a high probability of a highly valued reward. Bear in mind the buzz-name Victor Vroom, who formulated the theory.

2 The correct answer is **a**.

You ought to know Maslow's motivation theory well, and the quoted phrase is basic to that theory. Once a need is satisfied, it is no longer a need: however exhausted I am, once I have rested I no longer need rest, and the next set of needs will present itself. Unless you are very comfortable about your knowledge of Maslow, go back now to the Study Guide and check it out. The other authors named in the question are also absolutely central: check those too while you're about it.

3 The correct answer is **b**.

The clue to this is that *hygiene* factors have to do with what surrounds the job, factors in its work environment, and *motivators* to do with the job itself; *hygiene* with 'How am I treated', *motivators* with 'How am I used'. Apply this to the alternatives offered and you will find that all but the company rules are motivators. The name Herzberg (spell it right) should have been ringing in your brain, and you should be able to give a list of motivators/hygiene factors to prove you've studied him.

4 The correct answer is **a**.

Maslow again, folks, as we're sure you noticed. This is a very important need (as they all are if you have them) and one instinctively satisfied by many organizations, with club ties, social events, staff newspapers, interbranch competitions and so on. If you cannot satisfy it at work or at home, do understand that you may have to do it by putting on a football scarf once a week.

5 The correct answer is **d**.

Did you think 'McGregor'? If so, honestly, award yourself a bonus half-mark! Managers who hold the theory (Y) that people naturally want to work and create and achieve are more likely to gain a good response from the staff they wish to motivate than those who hold the theory (X) that they don't work unless forced. Remember that the Theories X and Y are in the mind-of-the-manager, not in the nature-of-the-world or the character-of-the-staff.

6 The correct answer is **c**.

Jobs are enriched by making them more complex or more responsible, adding *motivation* as opposed to *hygiene factors*. A wage rise is not usually job-enriching, except indirectly where it specifically relates to rewards for merit or for extra responsibility/complexity; and adding extra tasks of the same nature as those already performed is job-enlargement (extra half-mark for that too!). Telling people they are important is a good idea, if they believe it, and even job-enriching if related directly to the task.

7 The correct answer is **c**.

Length of service is no longer relevant to salaries (though age and qualifications on entry are; and service may affect holiday entitlement); the number of accounts at the branch are indirectly relevant because it is relevant to the grade of the managerial staff; industrial action is notoriously ineffective in wage-bargaining in UK clearing banks; but job evaluation is what it's all based on.

8 The correct answer is **a**.

Check the model in the study guide. If you're motivated you try harder; whether that leads to better performance is affected by a number of other things.

9 The correct answer is **d**.

You can indeed be demoted and earn *more* wages . . . . . and many Grade 1 incumbents earn more than those on Grade 2. this is because of the grade overlap, so that the top-end of one grade-band is higher than the bottom-end of the next one up. This allows for rises for excellence in one grade for people who would not necessarily do well in the next. It does not, by the way, logically entail that promotion will mean a drop, and no bank does that: they promote across or with a small congratulatory rise.

10   The correct answer is **b**.

That motivation is the drive to satisfy needs is simply and basically at the heart of sophisticated management theory. While there is a modicum of truth in the other statements, if you were to define motivation as any of them you would immediately give yourself away to the examiner as one of Nature's philosophers, a member of the 'What I always say is....' gang, and you would probably fail.

Score 2 marks for each correct answer. What was your score for this topic? Fill it in on the score grid.

If you scored 12 or less and are still a bit shaky on some points go back and look at the study guide again, before proceeding any further.

If you are sure you really understand and are familiar with the topic now, try the 10 further questions which are on pages 178-180.

Alternatively you can go on to the next topic and do all the post-tests together at the end.

Topic 8 Personnel Practices

Study guide

Case-study or straight questions on the headings under this topic are favourites with the examiners, because they can ask good practical questions about subjects with which you have had some contact, and they can expect systematic and sensible answers based on 'lists': so memorize some of the lists you will find below, and remember to state the principle or list and then apply it to the detail of the question, either point-by-point or principle-then-application.

No examiner likes moanings about personnel departments, who are generally not responsible for the various less-than-wonderful practices which abound in banks and elsewhere. As an examination candidate you must remember that personnel or staff departments have centralized (rather than operative) responsibility for the implementation and administration of personnel policies dictated to them from above, based on information collected by them from the organization.

They are not responsible for how well individual managers comply with organizational directives, formal or informal, concerning the treatment of staff, any more than the computer department is responsible for the manual competence of the terminal operator.

The point is important in this context because complaining about personnel departments, concerning how well or badly your staff are appraised, for example, or how they are selected for training, *gives you away* in examinations as naive, or lacking in study. Concentrate on proving to the examiner that you know about 'correct' principles, about the facts of how those are applied in your organization, or should be applied to the case in a case-study question, and only then add (objective) comment or criticism if it is asked for.

The headings we shall select for this chapter are as follows:

1 Manpower planning
2 Recruitment and selection
3 Induction
4 Training and development
5 Appraisal

Bear in mind that you need to be familiar with conventionally accepted theories of correct practice, and that it is additionally valuable to know your own system. It is *not* sensible to know your own system without the theory; and it is *even less sensible* to assume that your own bank's practices obtain throughout the industry, *or* that they are the best practices — remember that your paper can be marked by a manager in a rival or, anyway, a different bank!

Manpower planning

There's nothing like a good cliché to get you a mark: here's the one normally used to define Manpower Planning:

'The purpose of Manpower Planning is to see to it that the organization has the right people in the right jobs at the right time.'

The manpower plan, stating how many people we need, and with what training and experience, and of what calibre, will depend on what we plan to do. It is therefore, obviously, *derived from the corporate plan*. It usually has *short* or *medium term* elements (2–5 years) and *longer term* forecasts (up to 10 years); and if it is a sensible plan, it will be *flexible* enough to cope with unforeseen major changes in the banking scene (spot the three distinct marks this paragraph gives you. . .).

Manpower plans concern the *demand* for manpower, and the *supply* of it. You get points for this, and under Demand and Supply for mentioning some of the following; when looking at, and memorizing, these lists, think of the *reasons* for them and of *examples*:

Demand (depends on)	Supply (depends on)
Changes in organizational structure	
Changes in products/services	Current work force
Changes in market/environment	*less* wastage
Changes in legislation/government	*plus* recruitment
Changes in technology	
Wastage due to:	Age distribution
retirement	Sex distribution
death	Skills distribution
resignation	External education system
marriage	Labour market
childbearing	Image of banking
Changes due to promotion/moves	Recruitment policy

OK, have you thought of why supply and demand depend on these, and of examples? Don't go on until you've gone back and done that! This is because while the examiners like systematic lists, they do not like to think that you have parroted them without demonstrating understanding and insight, as future managerial Associates of the Institute of Bankers (quite rightly).

Recruitment and selection

These themselves depend on the manpower plan, and the systematic way (we hope) it is communicated to the recruitment section of your personnel department. They get to know how many people of what calibre are required to fill what jobs and by when, and then they enter the process which can be delineated with this list:

Job analysis and description	Of the post to be filled
Criteria set up	For appropriate candidate
Advertisement	Selecting correct media
Application form	Well designed and comprehensive
Selection interviews	Of those with good forms
Possible tests	Skill/intelligence/personality
Decision and offer	To criteria-fitters

As a revision exercise, think this list through for a particular post, say your own. Give thought to each stage, and jot down a few notes to expand on each point, as you will have to do in the exam if you answer a question on the recruitment process. If you have time, check out the appropriate paragraph in a personnel textbook to add to your jottings under each heading.

Note that banks normally still recruit at the bottom level, from school leavers at 16 or 18 years of age; but they also recruit graduates, specialists, senior executives and directors, and even branch managerial staff these days. Beware the phrase '*two* tier recruitment': banks engage in *multi-tier* recruitment, and all the former phrase meant was the idea of hiring some staff on a career path and some for specific low level jobs (which in truth, by the way, the banks have always done — think about it).

In the context of recruitment and selection there is something called the Seven Point Plan, which will get you marks. Set forward by the National Institute of Industrial Psychology, or NIIP, it concerns the headings under which criteria are set up (get that phrase right, and understand it) for selection, and is used for recruitment, or selection for management training, or even sometimes for appraisal. These are the seven points:

1	*Physical make up*	Health, appearance, speech, physique needed for post
2	*Attainment*	Previous experience, education, training for the job
3	*General intelligence*	What ability in reasoning needed to perform tasks
4	*Special aptitudes*	Amount of artistic, manual, verbal, numerate talents needed

5	*Interests*	Where relevant: hobbies likely to contribute to job-skills
6	*Disposition*	Personal traits and qualities, e.g. calmness, humour, courage
7	*Circumstances*	Background, family upbringing, financial, ties and dependants

Remember that much the same process is gone through when selecting people for promotion, or for management training, as for recruitment, and use the same models, adapted accordingly, if that is what the exam question asks.

Induction

Once recruited, the new employees need to be introduced to the organization, its ways and customs, its rules and regulations, its procedures and manners of work; and, quite importantly, to colleagues, supervisors or bosses, and other potentially significant people such as union representatives and personnel officers.

This can be done in a variety of ways, but essentially it should be done:

Early in the career, within the first few weeks
Divided between the workplace and other locations
By sensitive, reassuring trainers/other personnel
At a very basic level
Accompanied by plenty of useful handout material
In the company of other starters
With open, multiway communication

It would not be impossible for you to be asked to design an induction programme. You could state some or all of the above requirements, adding some of your own if you like, and then think of all that an entrant may need to know and set these down logically and sensibly, drawing on the better elements of your own induction experience (and even mentioning them if they — objectively — support your design argument).

Two additional points: not all recruits enter at school-leaver-junior level, and special induction may be needed for graduates or specialist experts; and included in induction programmes are, quite often, items of training for the basic elements of the job so that they do not start absolutely blind.

Training and development

In this subject there are several *pairs* of concepts to remember for your systematic answer to questions: these are

Training needs	The training gap
Objectives	Validation
Central/staff responsibility	Line responsibility
Organizational benefits	Staff benefits
On-the-job training	Off-the-job training
In-house training	External training
Management training	Technical training

Training needs/gap

A need for training has to be *diagnosed*, where people turn out to be less than competent, or when new skills are needed in individuals for their development, or in a group because of changed responsibilities, such as when a new service is introduced.

The measure of the extent of the training need is called the *training gap*: simply, the 'distance' or difference between the state of existing skills/knowledge (which has to be measured or tested) and that required to perform the tasks competently (which has to be projected and/or specified).

Training can then be devised to bridge the training gap.

Objectives/validation

In training as in every other managerial process it is important to have stated *objectives*. For every training experience, ideally, one should be able to find a statement in a manual or guide or timetable which states 'by the end of this training experience the candidate will be able to (or will be familiar with, or will know about). . .'.

This statement will enable the training designer to structure an appropriate experience; and it will allow for *validation*, because if you have a statement about what the candidate should be able to do after the course, you can test whether they can do it! It isn't quite as simple as that, and you may need pre-tests as well as post-tests, and you do need to know that the new skills were directly the result of the training (and not, for example, the maturing process or learnt elsewhere simultaneously).

Responsibility

Who is responsible for little Suzi's training?

The answer is little Suzi's boss. The training department is responsible for aiding and supporting the boss, by providing central resources, facilities, courses and administration. But discerning her need and readiness and ability to deal with the training experience is for the staff-member's immediate superiors to do.

In addition, for both technical and managerial training it is important to note that line management have the responsibility to supplement and embed the training in experience, by giving the candidate the opportunity to carry out in the workplace what has been learnt in the training.

There is one more seat of responsibility: in little Suzi herself, to take on the lessons and to put them into practice.

Training benefits

There are *organizational* benefits to training: across the whole organization, there are increased profits or savings, more flexibility in the face of the environment, a good succession of competent people into higher posts, a more motivated workforce.

At branch or section level, there is more likelihood that objectives will be achieved, that customers will have good service, that mistakes are minimized; and the manager has the ability to switch people from one task to another when needed.

The benefits to individual *staff members* of being well-trained lie in increased feelings of confidence and self-esteem, better promotion prospects, variety in their jobs, increased mobility from one job to another, and motivation.

On- or off-the-job training?

On-the-job training has the benefits of practicality and reality, cheapness, and supervision by people materially concerned. The drawbacks are the possibility that the 'trainer' operative is not necessarily competent, or uses non-recommended practices, or is a competent operative but a poor teacher, and there may be little or no reflection or feedback.

Off-the-job training might be courses or instruction manuals or video programmes or programmed learning texts. The benefits are in the protected environment, pure concentration on the learning process, trained trainers, properly planned and structured training experiences, reflection and feedback, and no risk of loss.

The ideal training process will include some of both, to absorb the pure theory on the one hand, and perfect correct techniques, and cement these at the workplace by practical, supervised experience.

127

In-house or external training

In-house and external training have some of the following advantages and disadvantages:

	Advantages	Disadvantages
In house	Unambiguous objectives	Narrow outlook
	Similar candidates	No cross-fertilization
	Convenient timing	Quality? No competition
	Lower variable cost	Close to home
	Familiar materials	
	Knowledgeable tutors	
External	Broader outlook	Incongruent objectives?
	Break from routine	High variable cost
	Competitive quality	Possible inappropriate
	Cross-fertilization	materials, content
	Unfamiliar candidates	Generalized objectives
	Fit into career gaps	

 Necessarily in note-form, these need expansion — in your mind: so go no further without thinking each and every one of the above through, and put yourself in the position of someone on a course inside and outside the organization; and if you think of any more to add to the list, add them in the margin (come on — how often are you going to use this book...?).

Technical/management training

All banks engage in sophisticated technical training, to ensure mechanical competence. Management training is more recent, developing over the last 10–15 years. Before that — and still in the minds of many — management training meant technical training for managers (Advanced Lending Courses and the like).

Nowadays it means training for managerial responsibility, and if you want to know what headings this comprises, either you shouldn't be taking an exam in the Nature of Management, or you could try the Contents pages of this book. Most banks now acknowledge that their managerial staff need to be technically competent and *separately* managerially trained/developed.

Please note that each bank has a different management training or development programme: the concept even means something different to each. So don't talk about 'the' management development programme or MDP as if it were common to all: refer to 'my bank's' MDP if required, describing it briefly for your examiner, who may work for one of the other banks, or for some other type of organization.

Appraisal

Similarly, every bank has a different appraisal system, and one of the best forms of revision for a possible question on appraisal in this paper is to get to know your own: the forms and the procedure.

You are practically bound to gain a mark in most questions on appraisal if you start by stating the *objectives* of an appraisal system:

For the organization	To adjust manpower plan
	To review stock of talent
	For promotions and moves
	To diagnose/anticipate problems
	To adjust training resources
For the appraiser	To sound out staff attitudes
	To motivate individual staff
	To adjust training
	To solve problems/grievances
	To review own performance
For the staff appraised	To obtain feedback about competence
	To remind of own achievements
	To remind of needed career moves
	To express own views on performance
	Obtaining guidance on improvement
	Reassurance and motivation

Most appraisal systems have a written and an interview element; some have a self-appraisal written component. Most are compulsorily annual, and have a compulsory or voluntary interim session.

In your examination there are what we might call 'standard expected comments', objective critical statements about appraisals, such as these, though beware of 'Barclaymoan', referring to the pain of your own experience:

An annual appraisal is too infrequent: managers forget what you did eleven months ago, and appraise you on the last three.

Continuous appraisal is the mark of the good manager: the annual session confirms what has been said all year round.

Appraisals suffer from personal bias: grades and comments depend on personal relationships.

Graders mark differently: you can suffer from 'hard' markers, or even known 'soft' markers; and personnel departments must know which is which.

Appraisals should be closely linked with counselling (see Topic 5, Communication) so that the candidate can devise methods for self-improvement under the appraiser's guidance.

Appraisers ought to, and sometimes don't, believe in the value of the system, not just pay lip-service to it.

Beware the 'halo-effect' (a well-known mark-acquiring cliche): if a candidate is good in one area (or pretty!) they will be marked well in others.

Appraisers are neither necessarily competent or well-trained.

Well-run appraisal systems are vital to the health of an organization, because they achieve the objectives suggested above.

As part of your revision you are heartily recommended to learn these and other such statements: starting from here, check out your textbooks and have your own set, listed and memorized. Appraisal in this context means *system*: if you can show the examiner that you know what it is for (*objectives*), how it is done (*forms/procedures*), and what you as a potential manager think about it (*critical comment*) properly applied to the question asked, you must have a pass answer.

Once you feel confident about your knowledge of this topic, try to answer the 10 multiple choice questions which follow.

Multiple choice questions

1 The manpower plan is derived from:

    a medium term strategic plans.
    b the annual Chairman's Statement.
    c the corporate plan.
    d the budget reports.

answer

2 The supply of manpower has nothing to do with:

    a the number of staff approaching retirement age.
    b governmental education policy.
    c the birth rate.
    d competition in the labour market.

answer

3 A job advertisement for a bank clerk should not detail:

    a the expected salary.
    b the sex of the ideal candidate.
    c expected educational qualifications.
    d expected career progression.

answer

4 Which of these is not usually of any relevance in the recruitment process:

    a physical fitness?
    b physiological attributes?
    c psychological testing?
    d psychoanalysis?

answer

5 One of the following is 'external training:

   a a Harvard Business School course.
   b a programmed learning text.
   c a residential course at the bank training centre.
   d a supervised reading programme.

answer

6 Which of the following has no share in young Donna's training:

   a young Donna?
   b The bank as a whole?
   c young Donna's immediate boss?
   d young Donna's branch manager?

answer

7 Management training is, most closely:

   a training managers to be technically superior.
   b theoretical confirmation of what managers already do.
   c making managers more worldly and outgoing.
   d training managers to perform managerial duties more effectively.

answer

8 Appraisal should be done:

   a annually.
   b six-monthly.
   c whenever the manager feels it necessary.
   d according to procedure.

answer

9 It is not necessary to include in a well-run appraisal procedure:

   a an interview.
   b a branch group-discussion of performance.
   c a self-appraisal of some form.

d plans for the ensuing period.

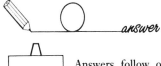 *answer*

10 In most organizations, personnel departments are responsible for:

    a the day to day performance of managers.
    b the day to day performance of staff.
    c the day to day manning levels of branches.
    d the standards of dress and grooming of personnel.

answer

Answers follow on pages 134-136. Score 2 marks for each correct answer.

Answers

1 The correct answer is **c**.

The corporate plan sets out the organization's intentions mainly concerning its activities in its environment or market. The implications for manpower needs are derived from that corporate plan, and, together with predictions as to the supply of labour, form the basis of the manpower plan. The other documents mentioned as alternative answers might indeed provide some information towards the manpower plan but are not its principal source.

2 The correct answer is **a**.

Strictly, if you count existing staff as part of the supply, then all of the answers suggested have to do with the supply of labour. However, retirement in fact provides fodder for the *demand* side principally, since as people retire they leave gaps to be filled. Do think of the manpower plan along an accounting analogy, if you like, where debit and credit must be balanced, or as an economic model where equilibrium is where Demand = Supply: matters of supply concern where fresh manpower is coming from; demand is where circumstances create a need to replenish.

3 The correct answer is **b**.

It cannot specify sex by law in any case, under the Sex Discrimination Act 1975; and it would not, since the UK clearing banks declared policies of equal pay and opportunities predating the law even of Equal Pay, 1970. Equal pay is now achieved, although some would debate assertions of the arrival of equal opportunity (see Topic 10, Industrial Relations).

4 The correct answer is **d**.

In most jobs a reasonable degree of physical fitness is required, though it is worth your being a little ingenious in making points like that and referring to company policies on the employment of a quota of disabled people, and the Disabled Persons (Employment); Act 1958. Physiological attributes are one of the points in the Seven Point Plan set forth by the NIIP — check the study guide. Psychological testing is more and more frequent in recent times, especially for graduates or for other candidates for managerial posts, from outside and within the organization. But psychoanalysis is not often used, though many would suggest of their colleagues that it should have been. . .

5 The correct answer is **a**.

Simply because a business school course takes place *outside the organization*. Don't confuse external training, which this is, with off-the-job training, which it also is because it takes place *away from the workplace*, as does the training in all the other answers.

6 The correct answer is **none of them**.

One mark if you selected any one: two only if you said that they all have a share: Donna herself must take responsibility for learning and putting what she has learnt into practice; the bank must provide training facilities and opportunities; the immediate boss must discern Donna's needs and apply for her training, and supervise its progress and effect; and the manager must programme the training of all branch staff (including the manager's own training), and must delegate and oversee the direct training efforts by the supervisors of the staff.

7 The correct answer is **d**.

Management training used to be equated with technical training for managerial staff. But in the last fifteen years or so in the UK banks it has been understood that training managers to be managers (of a bank) instead of (bank) managers meant training in all the topics covered in this volume. Management training can certainly have the effect of confirming theoretically the correctness of what good managers do well already, and of making them more wordly and and outgoing; but the closest definition is training to perform managerial duties more effectively.

8 The correct answer is **d**.

Try breaching your procedural regulations! (Not on *our* advice!). Your bank's procedure may call for annual or six-monthly appraisal, and there may be provision for occasional managerially-decided more frequent appraisals. In any case, the periodic appraisal session ought to be simply the formal part of a continuous, ongoing process of assessment and feedback, and it should be done competently and with specific training, as is done, for example, by the Royal Bank of Scotland.

9 The correct answer is **b**.

No elaboration needed! However, note that in the Red Army of China, a soldier's performance in an exercise is discussed in the open by officers and men; and then the officer's own performance is also discussed by all. There are some who might think that sort of thing an interesting addition to our appraisal systems. . .

10   The correct answer is **c**.

The rest are solidly the responsibility of line management.

Score 2 marks for each correct answer. What was your score for this topic? Fill it in on the score grid.

If you scored 12 or less and are still a bit shaky on some points go back and look at the study guide again, before proceeding any further.

If you are sure you really understand and are familiar with the topic now, try the 10 further questions which are on pages 180-182.

Alternatively you can go on to the next topic and do all the post-tests together at the end.

Topic 9   Groups

Study guide

Specific questions on concepts of group dynamics (which is what some textbooks call this topic) are rare; but many of the concepts can be included in a variety of answers, especially those couched in case-study terms: 'You have recently been appointed Assistant Manager of Downtown Branch. . . . . .'. Where the examiners are looking for knowledge of group theories, they expect brief but systematic statements of the principle, followed by applications, either to the case study or by use of examples from your own experience, to show that you have not only learnt words like 'boundaries' but understand their application.

This section will deal with

1 The concept of a group
2 Formal and informal groups
3 Group formation, development, and boundaries
4 Group norms
5 Conformity and sanctions
6 Communication patterns
7 Group leadership

The concept of a group

As we have seen in Topic 7 (Motivation), it was as a result of the Hawthorne Experiments that Elton Mayo (score an exam Brownie Point for mentioning either) publicized the fact that work is a group activity, and discovered that there were distinct behavioural effects of group membership: that is, when people join a group they behave differently from the way they do as individuals; and groups have different characteristics from simply collections of individuals.

Maslow emphasized people's social needs, to belong to groups; and Schein defined groups in a way that modern experts find acceptable, as:

'A number of people who interact with one another, are psychologically aware of one another, and perceive themselves to be a group' (more point-scoring).

How big is a group? The answer to this lies in two more buzzwords: the primary and the secondary group. The primary group is a small number, often quoted as 6–12, who constantly work together, such as the machine-room section of a branch. A secondary group is one whose members meet occasionally, such as a small number of section heads who have Monday Meetings, but not as a normal or constant part of the working week. Family and social groups are groups; but we shall be referring mostly to work groups, which are distinguished by having tasks or objectives.

Formal and informal groups

Another indicator to the examiner that you have studied this topic will be to know the difference between the formal and the informal group.

Formal groups

These are those set up and recognized by the organization, such as the staff at a sub-branch, the above-mentioned machine-room people, or a regional section in the personnel department. They exist to perform specific individual or long-running tasks for the organization.

Informal groups

These form by themselves within the organization, and could be groups of friends or people with similar interests. Membership can be roughly congruent with the formal group, or cut completely across boundaries. It may consist of all those who always go to the 'Dog and Partridge' for a drink on Fridays, or the girls who usually lunch at the far right corner of the canteen.

Organizational Behaviour, p. 134: Buchanan and Huczynski: Prentice Hall.

Most of the points which follow apply to both kinds of groups. It is important for management to be aware of the existence, membership, norms, sanctions, decision processes, communication and leadership of the informal as well as the formal group, because there are circumstances where the former is as strong or stronger as an influence on behaviour as those of the formal group.

Group formation and development; and boundaries

Formation

Formal groups are formed by the organization to pursue tasks. Informal groups come together for perceived common interests (good phrase), which may be — but aren't always — at odds with those of the organization; and may have their origins outside the organization, such as the group formed of neighbours from a particular commuter area, or of an age-group — the 'youngsters'. . . .

Development

A good simple model of the stages of development of a group is that of Tuckman, who suggested that group members come together and start by finding out who each other are, what they can do and how they behave, and they set out initial ways of working. They then get into a stage of conflict when adjustments have to be made and rivalries arise as to roles and responsibilities. When this is worked out, they develop new rules and methods, and finally they are in a position to produce really effective work and progress towards their objectives: as follows:

1 *Form* The coming-together, testing out of attitudes and abilities, working out initial roles and relationships.

2 *Storm* Conflict arising from adjustments to be made to the first agreements, often concerning leadership or control.

3 *Norm* Rules and norms of procedure and relationships have developed and progress begins to be made.

4 *Perform* Roles and relationships and procedures are stable and the group can concentrate its efforts on its aims and tasks.

The stages of Storm and Norm are sometimes reversed, even in textbooks: groups can get into a stable relationship before conflict arises. For examination purposes, however, if you use the model, reproduce the above ordering; and remember, state the principle and then give an example.

Organisational Behaviour, p. 141: Buchanan and Huczynski: Prentice Hall.

Boundaries

The group boundary is obviously the line drawn around the group defining who is in and who is outside it. Group conflict often concerns movement across the boundaries: groups have rules for admittance and for expulsion (*your* turn to think of examples, and write them down *now*, of each of an admittance and an expulsion rule for each of a formal and an informal group you know of).

Group norm

These are, broadly speaking, the rules of proper behaviour, or modus operandi, or principles of procedure with which the group agrees to operate. Norms can set production levels, as Mayo found out in the Hawthorne Experiments; or what language or slang words or nicknames are acceptable; or who sits at which desk, or who gets the next new chair, or even who we shall like or dislike or talk to or ignore.

When entering a new group, members need to 'find their way about', and this actually means learn the group norms, because if you don't, then acceptance as a full member will be impaired. Again, think *now* of examples of both stated and not-stated-but-expected norms from groups you know of, to break which would lead to awkwardness or even punishment.

Conformity and sanctions

Having rules and norms is one thing, enforcing them is something else. In many cases, rules don't need to be enforced, because group members are anyway inclined to conform. However, sometimes rules have to be pressed on people, and groups have methods of bringing the wayward back into line, and punishing those who deviate.

Conformity

Since the membership of an informal group is in any case probably voluntary, people have often joined *because* they wish to go the group way: their inclination to conform is almost by definition a qualification for membership.

But experiments by a man called Solomon Asch showed that when asked to agree or disagree with opinions expressed by the rest of their group, individuals would significantly often agree, against the evidence of their observations or what they actually see or believe. While this might have been because they actually doubted their own observation, it is more likely to have been the need to be liked and accepted that caused the agreement to be expressed.

This conformity is strengthened if the group consists of experts in its field and respected by each other, and if they are important to each other, and if each wishes to be like the others in many ways.

Sanctions

Despite the tendency to conform, groups have to have ways of disciplining wayward members to bring them into line with the rules. These tend to be progressive, starting with tacit disapproval, through explicit disapproval, removal of privileges and limiting shared information, through suspension (sending to Coventry) to expulsion. Think about these and apply them to possible situations in your own experience of both formal and informal groups.

 Organizational Behaviour, p. 173: Buchanan and Huczynski: Prentice Hall.

Communication patterns

No human enterprise succeeds for long without communication, but it cannot be assumed that all channels are always open, even within a small group. There has been plenty of research done on the most effective communication patterns, and while few groups actually construct themselves in these ways, the most familiar theories are those of Leavitt, who put people together in small groups so that they could only communicate in the patterns you see depicted below:

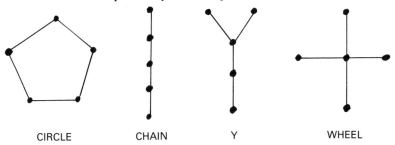

CIRCLE   CHAIN   Y   WHEEL

While (and this is hardly surprising) the Wheel pattern solved more problems more quickly, the Circle was slow, erratic but much more enjoyable. These diagrams may in fact get you marks in the exam, but even the author finds it hard to think of examples of how the findings can be applied to any real life situation, so don't bother!

The following are, however, important points:

The more effective the communication, the more effective the group. Communication is a large part of the responsibility of the leader.

The central communication focus-person, where there is one, was seen by members to be the leader of the group.

Group leadership

This will be dealt with at length as a separate topic. Here it is worth pointing out that group roles often have status attached to them, from the lowly through medium status to high, and the leader is always elected from the highest. **It is important to note** that the informal leader is by no means always the same person as the formal leader in the work situation: the latter can have been appointed by management, not realizing that that person is accorded low status by the informal group, who will then look to the informal leader for confirmation of instruction or commands.

It is well, therefore, for management to know of the informal status and leadership system, and take account of it in appointing acceptable people to high formal positions, and use it sometimes diagnostically where there seem to be leadership problems.

These are not all the concepts and models used in group dynamics, but they are central; check out your textbooks for more, if you like. Remember to score exam points by stating the name of the concept, preferably with capital letters ('Group Norms'); cite the authors ('Solomon Asch'); think of examples to illustrate, *during your revision period* rather than leaving it to hope something will occur to you during the examination — though of course it may — and reproduce diagrams wherever possible for extra scoring.

Once you feel confident about your knowledge of this topic, try to answer the 10 multiple choice questions which follow.

Multiple choice questions

1 Which of the following is not usually seen to be part of the development of a gorup:

   a   forming?
   b   norming?
   c   reforming?
   d   storming?

 answer

2 Which of the following needs is a group leader said to try and satisfy:

   a   individual needs?
   b   economic needs?
   c   self-actualization needs?
   d   hierarchical needs?

 answer

3 According to Schein, which of the following does not necessarily contribute to the definition of a group:

   a   they intract with each other?
   b   they are psychologically aware of each other?
   c   they perceive themselves to be a group?
   d   they have a high degree of respect for each other?

 answer

4 Of the following statements, which is true of an informal group:

   a   it is set up by the management?
   b   its main purpose is social?
   c   it creates its own rules for its members?
   d   it always defies the organization's objectives?

 answer

5 In Leavitt's experiments, which of these formations of group communication did he not try:

   a the square formation?
   b the 'Y' formation?
   c the circle formation?
   d the chain formation?

6 One of the following is likely to be described as an example of a 'group norm':

   a having to wear ties for social meetings.
   b expressing a preference for tall men.
   c refraining from smoking during group meetings.
   d always letting the older members speak first.

7 How big is a group?

   a 6–10 people
   b 4–7 people?
   c any size above 3 people?
   d any size that perceives itself to be a group?

8 Who developed ideas concerning work being a group activity:

   a Abraham Maslow?
   b Elton Mayo?
   c Henry Mintzberg?
   d Malcom Marshall?

9 A group boundary is:

   a a high-scoring achievement by the group?
   b the edges of the group's premises?

Topic 9 Multiple choice: *Questions*

c the definition of who is and is not a member?

d limits the group puts on its members' behaviour?

answer

10 Which of these would not happen to Helen as a *direct* result of Helen trangressing her informal group's rules:

a she could be expelled?

b she would be fired?

c she could be reprimanded?

d she could be sent to Coventry?

answer

Answers follow on pages 146-148. Score 2 marks for each correct answer.

Answers

1 The correct answer is **c**.

Groups may indeed reform after problems, but that term is not usually used, and you should have memorized, in the correct order, form, storm, norm, perform. Try the model out in any small group or project team you've been a member of — you will probably find it an accurate relating of how the group developed.

2 The correct answer is **a**.

Individual needs are one of the three sets of group needs which, according to John Adair's Action-Centred Leadership model, a leader has to satisfy. The phrase 'satisfying group needs' should have been a clue to you and you can give yourself an extra half-mark if Adair or the three-circle model occurred to you — and deduct one if you haven't the faintest idea what I'm on about. And if so, back to Topic 6 with you!

3 The correct answer is **d**.

While members of the group may have respect for each other, frankly they may define themselves as a group even if they do not. This is a good example of the need to read the question carefully, because it did not ask about the effectiveness of groups, which might well depend on respect; it asked about definition of a group. The whole question relates to Schein's definition, and he is an important social psychologist; it is one of the few definitions which are widely accepted. Check it out, learn it, and get an extra mark by quoting it and Schein in the examination.

4 The correct answer is **c**.

It is by definition *not* set up by management, but by its own members regardless of management structures; its main purpose may be social, but it may be a number of other things, like defiance, or friendship, or to pursue specific objectives that the members have; informal groups do not always defy organizational objectives, though they can if they decide to; but the creation of its own rules is a central defining factor for the informal group.

5 The correct answer is **a**.

If he had tried the square, the effect would have been the same as for the circle: look up the diagram in the study guide to work out why that is. But *before* you do, try and remember what that effect would be — what were the characteristics of communication in the circle formation?

6 The correct answer is **b**.

Group norms are informal, usually unwritten rules of behaviour which, if breached, lead to some form of disapproval or sanction or punishment from the group. So if we 'usually, old chap' wear ties to the meetings, or 'hope you don't smoke at the meetings, Gail — the rest of us don't', or 'always let the seniors tell us what they think before we say anything', then you had better comply or we won't be happy with you. But unless the gorup is specifically a tall-man-fancying club, your actual preferences may not disqualify you from approval.

7 The correct answer is **d**.

Some say that a 'small group' for purposes of social science investigations is rarely more than 6–10 people; but in Schein's definition, number is less important than self-identification.

8 The correct answer is **b**.

Maslow was less interested in group activity than in motivation in social environments; Mintzberg concerned himself with the role and functions of the manager; Marshall is a West-Indies cricketer of spectacular accomplishment, whose theories on social psychology, however, are unknown to the author of this volume; but after his work on the Hawthorne Experiments — seek them out and read about them back in Topic 1 — Mayo and his associates developed important thinking about working in groups.

9 The correct answer is **c**.

The group boundary is the definition of who is in and who is out, and has rules attached about who may cross in, or out, temporarily or permanently, and how and with what qualifications people may join.

10 The correct answer is **b**.

Since the informal group is not set up by the organization, Helen could not be fired as a direct result of her misbehaviour. The group could make her continued employment uncomfortable for her, and could conspire to put her in difficult situations with the boss, or even dishonestly 'frame' her with company misdemeanours so that she would be vulnerable to dismissal procedures. But informal groups have a progressive arsenal of sanctions they could apply, and the other multiple-choice answers name some of them; getting Helen fired would probably be a last and most extreme set of actions, albeit within the group's capability.

Score 2 marks for each correct answer. What was your score for this topic? Fill it in on the score grid.

If you scored 12 or less and are still a bit shaky on some points go back and look at the study guide again, before proceeding any further.

If you are sure you really understand and are familiar with the topic now, try the 10 further questions which are on pages 182-184.

Alternatively you can go on to the next topic and do all the post-tests together at the end.

Topic 10   Industrial Relations

Study guide

Questions under this topic are really quite frequently asked, although it doesn't appear in the Syllabus as such: what is referred to is 'Sources of Potential Conflict'. The heading will cover, for our purposes,

1 Collective bargaining
2 Trades unions in banking
3 Employment legislation
4 Consultation and participation systems
5 Grievance and discipline
6 Negotiation

Most practising managers have little to do with the formal systems of industrial relations; but it forms the background to managerial actions and decisions, and that is why it is included and tested as part of your AIB qualifications. Besides that, the statement is not entirely true in that certain parts of the formal system do turn up in the office, either in the shape of personnel procedures or Office Representatives, and even the occasional local or national dispute.

The probability is that familiarity with industrial relations matters as here defined, coupled with a knowledge of how they are implemented in your bank, gives you a good chance of passing one question on your Nature of Management paper.

Collective bargaining

Means what it says: a collection of one set of people bargain with a collection of another set, usually by using representatives and usually employers on the one hand and employees on the other.

Traditionally in the UK the element of fairness to both sides has been achieved through what might be referred to as cooperative conflict, bargaining largely with goodwill between groups who are seeking the largest reasonable benefit for themselves or those they represent.

In this topic, do remember this goodwill, and the fact that conflict is constructive in this context. Examiners are irritated by anti-union opinions, especially from you who are quite likely to be fully-paid-up members of your union in an industry which encourages a high level of union membership for reasons we will lay out below.

Note that collective bargaining is an important communication device, in which the wishes and aspirations and plans of management and of workers are made known to each other for the sake of organizational advance. Much of what follows in the next section can be used in any question which makes reference, or in which you make reference, to collective bargaining.

Trades unions in banking

While most get this right in examinations, many have strange ideas about the history of, and bank and staff attitudes towards, union membership. In fact, since the last really effective strike (for union recognition in 1967), there has been an agreed system of collective bargaining largely favoured by both sides.

Banks are in favour of sensible trade union activities; the majority of dealings between employers and unions are positive and effective; the largest banking union, though affiliated to the TUC, is non-political; and a majority of bank staff are members of a union or similar organization.

Examiners don't like naive political stances in the exam. Whatever your deeply held views on either side of the political spectrum, these are rarely if ever required: just an understanding of the nature and processes of employer/union activity, and their importance to the manager.

History of union representation

Early 20th century to 1946: Bank Officers' Guild

1946: Became National Union of Bank Employees (NUBE); still about half bank employees members of individual banks' staff associations and not unions.

1967–68: NUBE National Strike to achieve recognition by employers; immediate subsequent foundation of national negotiating machinery called the Joint Negotiating Council: employers and union and staff associations.

1973: Midland Bank Staff Association transferred membership to the Association of Scientific, Technical and Managerial Staffs Union (ASTMS).

1979: NUBE bcame Banking, Insurance and Finance Union (BIFU).

Late 1970s: Dr T. Johnston's attempts to bring BIFU and staff associations together failed.

1980: Staff associations combine to become Clearing Banks Union (CBU), unlike BIFU not affiliated TUC.

The main difference between BIFU and CBU is an attitude: the former is for constructive conflict and behaving like a traditional UK trade union; the latter for cooperation with management and behaving like a traditional professional association.

There is a formal system of collective bargaining between the Federation of London Clearing Banks Employers (FLCBE) and each of the large unions separately (but usually identically); and each bank has also a mechanism for local agreement.

The situation, of rivalry and failure to agree as between the *unions*, is problematic; is not to the liking of many ordinary members; causes delays in implementing agreements; and is the subject of frequent attempts to resolve, both from outside and within.

At one time, either side could call in binding arbitration independently, but because of the fear of the possibility of the abuse of this — with no particular historical example — the FLCB unilaterally withdrew from this and now arbitration is only possible with the agreement of both sides.

Revision

You are encouraged to know the bare facts as outlined here. But remember that *this topic is topical*: things can change between writing and publishing, and between your buying and reading this book. Keep up to date by reading your trade press (the *Financial Times*, *Banking World*, your union newspaper, your bank's staff journal).

If you are an overseas student, you can usually choose to answer questions using the UK facts, or use the facts of your own country of domicile. It has frankly historically been more effective for overseas students to avoid trying to answer a question on industrial relations situations in which they have never been involved.

Employment legislation

You will not be required to be expert in the detail of employment legislation; nevertheless it is useful to know that there is legislation relating to:

Trades union representation, giving rights to be or not to be a member, and laying down rules for the foundation and conduct of closed-shop agreements, such as those in Tesco, United Biscuits, the press and film industries.

Employment protection, establishing legal rules for employment, suspension, fair and unfair dismissal, maternity rights, redundancy and appeal.

Equal opportunity, both with relation to race and to sex.

And such topics as *Health and Safety at Work,* and *Shops, Office and Railway premises,* and *Insurance* and so on.

Again, avoid expressing *opinions* on some of these somewhat controversial topics (you don't usually get asked what you *think of* legislation, so it wouldn't be answering the question anyway): what you consider to be a mild and sensible personal comment on the negative aspects of maternity leave, for example, may read unfavourably to the pregnant lady assistant manager who is marking your paper. . . .

Consultation and participation systems

These terms can be problematic, but they usually mean ways of employers and staff communicating corporately to share in decisions, often but not necessarily outside the union processes.

Three points may get you examination marks under this heading:

1 Mandatory consultation: employers are obliged by law to consult employees on Health and Safety (H. and S. Act 1974) and on redundancy (various employment protection Acts).
2 The Bullock Committee: a committee of enquiry set up under Sir Alan (now Lord) Bullock worked from 1975 to 1978 to obtain evidence about worker participation. Its main conclusion, that there should be worker directors on the boards of public companies, was very favourably received and extremely rarely acted upon. . .
3 Domestic consultation/participation systems: certain banks have systems of consultation and participation, mobilizing staff talents and opinions on a variety of matters.

One of the best-known (and often quoted in answers) was the William & Glyn's (now Royal Bank of Scotland) scheme. This consisted of a top level committee of representatives from all areas of the bank, meeting monthly and producing a report for all staff; and quarterly participation meetings of all units (branches, offices, sections) conveying staff views upwards to the executive.

If your own bank has such a scheme — and they have various names

— outline its details. There are possible marks in objective (I said *objective*!) criticism, such as comments on the dependence of success on the commitment, enthusiasm and competence of local management and staff.

By the way, note the distinction, not always made in this industrial-relations context, between consultation (management asks but then decides) and participation (everybody decides).

Grievance and discipline

In any human organization there will be times when the individual is unhappy about the organization — will entertain a *grievance* — and when the organization is not satisfied with the behaviour of the individual — will need to apply *discipline*.

In such sophisticated organizations as banks, there should be properly laid down procedures to handle both types of situation, and indeed there are.

Distinction should be made between *informal* and *formal* discipline and grievance procedures. 'Grievances' and 'disciplinary matters' can often, and should usually or anyway initially, be dealt with locally, informally, by a complaint to the manager or a telling-off for the staff member.

You shouldn't ignore the mark to be gained by making that point, going on to note that the formal 'procedures' are only invoked after it has become locally impossible to deal with the problem. These procedures are thankfully rarely used, but their existence ensures fair treatment for both parties. It should be made clear and in writing, by the way, to the object of the procedure when that procedure has been started in relation to them.

Both *grievance* and *disciplinary* procedures should be:

— Written: they will be complex and detailed
— Clear and understandable, with clear rules of progress
— Logically constructed with one step leading to the next
— Time-limited, to deal quickly and efficiently with the problem
— Allowing for either party to be represented by union or association
— Equipped with appeal procedures after decision

Grievance procedures should be:

— Accessible to anyone with a grievance
— Specific in who can deal with what sort of grievance

Disciplinary procedures should be:

— Fair and seen to be fair to all parties

153

— Specific in: what behaviours are/are not permitted
                  what penalties attach to what misdemeanour
                  what disiplinary powers lie where

 As a revision exercise, go about trying to find out how the grievance and disciplinary procedures are invoked in your bank, and what are their nature and general provisions. If they are any good you should be able to do this easily! You may be well-advised to tell your superiors why you are doing this, by the way. . .

Negotiation

Negotiation is included under this topic because, though it is just a formalized method of human interaction, it is most often used in industrial relations or formal conflict matters. It is not just limited to major matters of national agreement, but can be engaged in, say, by your manager negotiating a commission rate with a corporate customer.

Remembering the examiners' love of lists — they make answers so much easier to mark *in themselves* as well as because they demonstrate your study, your knowledge and your systematic approach — note and learn that negotiations have certain *defining elements* and go through *phases*.

Defining elements

Negotiations are characterized as follows:

— There are two or more parties with differing interests
— All parties want eventual agreement
— All parties want the best deal for their party
— There is power on both sides
— The power is not unbalanced too much one way or the other
— There are constraints and limits on both sides
— The negotiators usually represent large bodies
— The negotiation is usually time-constrained
— Strategy, tactics, skills and pscyhology are involved
— There are rules and rituals of behaviour

Think these through, with relation **both** to the GLCBE and the unions negotiating the annual pay-rise, *and* to your manager and his corporate customer: your revision should not just involve learning (and adding, if you like, to) these lists, but understanding them too.

Phases

Negotiations tend to go through the following stages:

— The *opening phase*: jockeying for position
— The *exploratory phase*: finding out where the opening positions are
— *Confrontation*: attacking the other side's opening position
— *Clarification*: finding out what leeway there is on either side
— *Bargaining phase I*: suggesting less-painful concessions
— *Bargaining phase II*: trading real concessions to reach agreement
— *Agreement*: publication and implementation

Negotiation is a fascinating ritual process and you would be well advised, as well as finding it interesting, to check out a chapter on it in your textbooks — they may differ from the above (since they all differ from each other) in their descriptions both of definition elements and of phases.

But remember that the examiners are looking at your paper with whatever marking scheme they have on the one hand, their view of a sensible and systematic approach to answers, especially in the Nature of Management, on the other — and, finally, an eye on their clock and a whole bunch of other people's disorganized papers still to mark...

Once you feel confident about your knowledge of this topic, try to answer the 10 multiple choice questions which follow.

Multiple choice questions

1 One of the following sets of initials has no connection with bank staff representation:

   a CBSA.
   b CPSU.
   c CBU.
   d BIFU.

2 On which of the following pieces of legislation is there mandatory consultation between staff and employees:

   a Employment Protection Act?
   b Sale of Goods Act?
   c the Health and Safety at Work Act?
   d Equal Opportunities Act?

3 The Association of Scientific, Technical and Managerial Staffs represents employees in one of the UK clearing banks:

   a Lloyds.
   b Royal Bank of Scotland.
   c Barclays.
   d Midland.

4 Bank employers and staff negotiate on all but one of the following:

   a holidays.
   b sickness benefits.
   c salaries, Grades 1–4.
   d working hours.

5   Which of the following bodies is affiliated to the TUC:

   a   the Banking, Insurance and Finance Union?
   b   the Clearing Banks Union?
   c   the Federation of London Clearing Banks Employers?
   d   the National Westminster Staff Association?

6   Which of these does not characterize a 'negotiation':

   a   both parties want the best possible deal?
   b   the parties usually represent larger bodies of people?
   c   either party will hold out until victory?
   d   there are formal or informal rules of behaviour?

7   Banks are said to offer equal opportunities to men and women. In
   the light of that, what proportion of Managerial Appointed Staff in
   the four major UK clearing banks are women? Approximately:

   a   3%–5%.
   b   10%–12%.
   c   25%–30%.
   d   50%.

8   As part of a disciplinary procedure, for which of the following
   might you expect that summary dismissal would be the penalty:

   a   persistent lateness?
   b   being caught stealing from the bank?
   c   gross impertinence to superior officers?
   d   demonstrable incompetence?

9   Which of these would you expect to be the first step in a
   disciplinary procedure:

   a   a written warning?
   b   a confidential report to the personnel department?
   c   a reprimand by Regional Head Office?
   d   a verbal warning?

 _answer_

10   With which political party are the CBU and BIFU aligned:

   a   the Labour Party?
   b   the Conservative Party?
   c   the Liberal/SDP Alliance?
   d   none of these?

 _answer_

 Answers follow on pages 159-161. Score 2 marks for each correct answer.

Answers

1 The correct answer is **b**.

The CBSA is — or rather was — the Clearing Banks Staff Associations, which became the CBU, the Clearing Banks Union; and BIFU is the Banking, Insurance and Finance Union. The CPSU is the Civil and Public Service Union.

2 The correct answer is **c**.

Despite the daily press's standard view, industrial relations in the UK are usually sound and harmonious, and consultation takes place voluntarily between staff and employers' bodies on a number of matters where neither the law nor the standard negotiating agreements bind them to do so. It is possible, therefore, for all the named pieces of legislation to be a matter for consultation, and it could be argued that they would be in a healthy relationship. However, it is legally mandatory only in the case of the Health and Safety at Work Act.

3 The correct answer is **d**.

In Lloyds and Barclays, both BIFU and the CBU represent staff; in the Royal Bank of Scotland BIFU has sole negotiating rights; in the Midland, there is the CBU, BIFU and ASTMS, but the last-named has in fact no negotiating rights.

4 The correct answer is **b**.

See again the answer to Question 2. Though sickness benefits are not an officially negotiable matter, this does not prevent the parties discussing reasonable levels of benefit if there is any problem. Check out, however, the list of negotiable matters: it's a good point-scoring ploy for the exam.

5 The correct answer is **a**.

When NUBE, now BIFU, became affiliated to the TUC, a letter to the *Banking Magazine* from an assistant manager in one of the older banks described it as a 'dangerous swerve to the Left'! Now, because of the size of membership, the General Secretary of BIFU has a seat on the TUC General Council, and would claim to provide a healthy moderate voice on that body. Neither BIFU nor CBU have connections or affiliations with any political party, or any party political views, though

ASTMS is closely aligned with the Labour Party and is also affiliated to the TUC.

6 The correct answer is **c**.

If either party is determined to hold out until victory, there can be no negotiation: for an example of this, look at the Miner's Strike of the early 1980s, when *both* sides decided to hold out until victory — negotiation hardly entered the range of behaviours engaged in. True negotiation certainly includes conflict, and a desire for the best possible deal, and even 'victory'; but it is characterized by genuine desire for agreement as the eventual outcome.

7 The correct answer is **a**.

You're not surprised, are you, that the proportion is 3–5% (and nearer 3%)? But nearer 60% of bank staff are women; well over 5% of AIBs are women, and that is double the number in 1978; and every year some 20%–25% of the Top 50 at Institute of Bankers Diploma level are female. You have already been warned in the Study Guide to beware of expressing your *views* about the actual state of female emancipation in banking during your exam: the examiner may well be one of those lady AIBs, and if you're sexist you'll get the bias you deserve! Beware also of your social theories for the *reasons* for low numbers of ladies in higher grades, unless you have published them in a reputable journal or can show yourself to have gained them by study. Nothing gives away the naive, unschooled exam-taker better than global theories without statistical or well-read backing, and you'll attract the contempt of the examiner of whatever sex.

8 The correct answer is **b**.

Summary dismissal means on the spot, no warning or notice, and with immediate effect. You can be so fired for being caught stealing. You can also be fired for the other offences, but only 'fairly dismissed' after the full process of the disciplinary procedure has been carried out. You could quote the content of (though you'll get away with a mark for the *name* of) the Employment Protection (Consolidation) Act 1978, which deals with fair and unfair dismissal, though this first appeared in the Industrial Relations Act of 1971.

9 The correct answer is **d**.

You'll know because you have read Topic 5 that by a verbal warning we really mean an oral warning (with the mouth!). The other alternative answers may form part of the procedure, and in the case of ignorant or less-than-courageous managers, they may even precede addressing the naughty staff member. But it would be normal procedural practice, and certainly sound managerial practice, for the first steps in discipline to be an interview, possibly culminating in a personal warning, from superior to subordinate.

10 The correct answer is **d**.

The banking unions are scrupulous in their insistence on not being affiliated to political parties. BIFU is in fact affiliated to the TUC, claiming to be a moderate voice in its counsels; and because of the size of the membership, the General Secretary of BIFU has a seat on the TUC General Council. However, this does not indicate any political bias.

Score 2 marks for each correct answer. What was your score for this topic? Fill it in on the score grid.

If you scored 12 or less and are still a bit shaky on some points go back and look at the study guide again, before proceeding any further.

If you are sure you really understand and are familiar with the topic now, try the 10 further questions which are on pages 185-187.

Alternatively you can go on to the next topic and do all the post-tests together at the end.

Post-tests

Pages 164-187 contain 10 further multiple
choice questions for each topic.

Questions

Topic 1   Organizations

1   Which of the following said 'The decisive reason for the advance of bureaucratic organisation has always been its purely technical superiority over any other form of organisation':

   a   Joan Woodward?
   b   Henri Fayol?
   c   Freddie Laker?
   d   Max Weber?

2   In which decade were the Hawthorne Experiments largely carried out:

   a   1920–1930?
   b   1900–1910?
   c   1940–1950?
   d   1930–1940?

3   According to systems theory which of the following would be an 'input' to a banking system:

   a   an insurance package for mortgage protection?
   b   staff salaries and wages?
   c   capital raised by the bank's own rights issue?
   d   the bank's advertising campaign?

4   Which of the following does not characterize a principle of organization as suggested by the Classical School:

   a   the scalar chain?
   b   the parity principle?
   c   the span of control?

164

d the quality of mercy?

 answer

5 In which of the following ways of representing an organization is the line and staff relationship most clearly depicted:

a matrix?
b concentric?
c hierarchical?
d directory?

 answer

6 According to Joan Woodward, what sort of a management structure might a private architect's office have:

a flexible?
b rule-bound?
c specialized?
d predictable?

 answer

7 Which of the following might be described as a 'charismatic' leader:

a Arthur Scargill?
b Napoleon Buonaparte?
c Margaret Thatcher?
d all of them?

 answer

8 In which of the following schools of thought would the concept of 'group dynamics' be most likely to be used:

a systems thinking?
b human relations
c scientific management?

d classical school?

9 'Contingency' is most closely defined as:

a coping with emergencies on the spot.
b where one organization is situated close to another.
c the best form of organization for its environment.
d having good relationships with other organizations.

10 Which of the following might be described by Burns and Stalker as 'organic':

a the administration department of a school?
b the grading system of your bank?
c the General Synod of the Church of England?
d the buying staff of a fashion boutique?

Topic 2   The banking environment

1 Which of the following is a demographic description:

a she's a tall and elegant lady?
b she enjoys being the centre of attention?
c she is a member of the urban peasantry?
d she is intelligent but lazy-minded?

2 Which of these competes with clearing banks as a lender of funds to private individuals for house-purchase:

a the Post Office?
b the building societies?
c the Department of Health & Social Security?

d the Bank of England?

answer

3 Which of these is an important principle in Labour Party policy:

   a progressive personal taxation?
   b unilateral nuclear disarmament?
   c widespread share ownership?:
   d private education for all?

answer

4 What percentage of the population of Great Britain and Northern Ireland is non-Caucasian (Asian & Afro-Caribbean):

   a 10%?
   b 20%?
   c 35%?
   d 5%?

answer

5 What educational achivement do you need to put you in the top 20% of the UK population:

   a 2 'A'-levels?
   b 8 'O'-levels?
   c 4 'O'-levels?
   d a degree?

answer

6 Which of these does not describe a particular modern machine now in fairly common use in business:

   a VDU?
   b ATM?
   c JCB?
   d PC?

answer

7 Which bank has been 'privatized':

   a Post Office Savings?
   b Trustee Savings?
   c Citibank?
   d the Bank of England?

 _answer_

8 'A central computer with remote multiple terminals': this describes:

   a a mainframe computer?
   b a microcomputer?
   c a personal computer?
   d an electronic computer?

 _answer_

9 Which of the following can be obtained from a UK clearing bank:

   a government grants?
   b loans to finance gun-running?
   c shares in quoted companies?
   d advice on personal taxation?

 _answer_

10 Which of the following is least likely to be involved in discussions of mergers of major public companies:

   a the Monopolies Commission?
   b the Office of Fair Trading?
   c the Department of Employment?
   d the Department of Trade & Industry?

 _answer_

Topic 3   Managerial roles and processes

1   'The way a role should be performed according to the others in the role set' is:

   a   the role requirements.
   b   the role specification.
   c   the role expectations.
   d   role ambiguity.

 *answer*

2   A role set is:

   a   a collection of similar roles.
   b   all the roles in a play.
   c   all the roles contiguous with a focal role.
   d   a collection of complementary roles.

 *answer*

3   Which of these is an interpersonal role, in Mintzberg's model:

   a   leader?
   b   negotiator?
   c   disseminator?
   d   disturbance handler?

 *answer*

4   Which of these is part of the managerial process:

   a   discipline?
   b   counselling?
   c   appraisal?
   d   control?

 *answer*

5   According to Belbin, the team role responsible for harmony in the group is called:

a shaper.
b team worker.
c company worker.
d finisher.

6 The bank manager's impressive leather topped desk is:

a a role-expectation.
b a role-depictor.
c a role-sign.
d a role-mop.

7 Setting stages in a project and checking progress against them is:

a planning.
b organizing.
c motivating.
d controlling.

8 Motivation is:

a a significant part of the managerial process.
b the first step in the managerial process.
c a side-issue as far as the managerial process is concerned.
d no part of the managerial process.

9 Forecasting is based largely upon:

a best estimates by experienced managers.
b the theories of business academics.
c the analysis of past trends.

d the predictions of financial press experts.

10 'Organizing' is the present tense of:

    a history.
    c planning.
    c controlling.
    d accountancy.

Topic 4   Managerial techniques and tools

1 Which of these would be most likely to fall into the market segment of clearing banks:

    a the unemployed?
    b the criminal classes?
    c employees of the Bank of England?
    d employees of ASDA supermarkets?

2 Consumer research differs from market research because:

    a it is less rigorous.
    b it concerns only customers of services being researched.
    c it is always done in the street.
    d it is a commercial activity done by paid researchers.

3 Which of these is a demographic factor, statistics of which are freely available:

    a the population age-breakdown?
    b information concerning the medical record of people?
    c preferences concerning styles of footwear?

d the possible whereabouts of missing persons?

4 Which of theese characterizes *group* as opposed to *individual* decision making:

a it is faster?
b it is more economical?
c it is always more enjoyable to most people?
d it generates more alternative courses of action?

5 When you have decided on the solution to a problem you must:

a implement actions to cope with it.
b hand the responsibility to a subordinate.
c actively seek out more problems.
d indicate your success to your superiors.

6 CPA stand for:

a Catering Packages Associates.
b Clearing Practices for Accountants.
c Critical Path Analysis.
d Collections of Possible Actions.

7 Program Evaluation Review Technique is:

a a technique for evaluating computer programs.
b a technique for efficient project planning/management.
c a technique of evaluating viewer figures for TV programmes.
d a technique for estimating the cost of projects.

8 Management by objectives:

    a has nothing to do with the reward system.
    b rewards those who formulate and set objectives.
    c punishes managers who fail to reach targets.
    d contributes reward to managers who reach objectives.

9 The main British exponent of management by objectives is:

    a John Adair.
    b John Humble.
    c John Gummer.
    d John Bell.

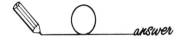

10 'Making predictions about the future course of events' is:

    a organizing.
    b forecasting.
    c planning.
    d diagnosis.

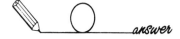

Topic 5   Communication

1 In the traditional communication model, the person who thinks up a message to send is called the:

    a transmitter.
    b originator.
    c source.
    d sender.

2 Noise is:

    a sounds which interfere with oral messages.
    b environmental factors distracting from meanings of messages.
    c a fault in the message making it unintelligible.
    d emotional problems which interfere with interpretation.

3 Which of these could act as a psychological barrier to communication:

    a the recipient having a tendency to nervous breakdown.
    b the Post Office van having a tendency to break down.
    c the electronic transmitter breaking down.
    d the breakdown of negotiations between bank and staff.

4 One of these would be described as a semantic problem:

    a failing to see a road sign in the dark.
    b failing to see distress in a lonely friend.
    c not understanding why he lost his temper.
    d 'But, for mine own part, it was Greek to me. . . . . .'

5 To plan an interview, you *must* compose in advance:

    a your features.
    b your questions.
    c your demeanour.
    d your exit line.

6 An interview should be:

    a controlled.
    b informal.
    c short.

d during working hours.

7 'Grasping your own brief' necessitates:

a maintaining a hold on your script.
b keeping your brief secret until published.
c understanding every element of the project.
d keeping control of the staff on the project.

8 For an efficient and effective session, during a briefing the staff should be encouraged to:

a remain silent unless they cannot hear.
b remain silent unless they object to the actions proposed.
c interrupt to ask for clarification.
d interrupt to make alternative proposals.

9 A PIN is:

a a Personal Identification Number.
b a Private Identification Number.
c a Personal Informational Nomenclature.
d a useful device for attaching things together.

10 Which of these collects, sorts and retrieves material in a similar way to a card index system:

a a word processor?
b a spreadsheet?
c a Winchester disk?
d a database package?

Topic 6   Leadership

1   What is impoverished management:

    a   management on low pay?
    b   a style at 1,1 on the grid?
    c   management with few creative ideas?
    d   management only interested in output?

2   The managerial grid was designed by:

    a   Burns & Stalker.
    b   Lawrence & Lorsch.
    c   Blake & Mouton.
    d   Holmes & Watson.

3   John Adair's is a leadership model which is depicted by:

    a   a triangle with lateral layers.
    b   triangles with 'linking pins'.
    c   three overlapping circles.
    d   a horizontal line with gradations.

4   Select the phrase which best describes the consultative style:

    a   manager consults group and takes own decisions.
    b   manager consults group and implements their decisions.
    c   manager consults group and ignores advice.
    d   manager consults group on important decisions.

5   The main theorist of ideas on situational leadership was:

    a   Elizabeth Barrett Browning.
    b   Susan Fleur Hudson.

    c   Helen Bradley Zimmer.

    d   Mary Parker Follett.

 answer

6 Arthur Fiedler was responsible for ideas about:

    a   a theory of effective leadership.

    b   a theory of action centred leadership.

    c   a theory of situational leadership.

    d   a theory of charismatic leadership.

 answer

7 According to Reddin, a bureaucrat is a manager who:

    a   is low on effectiveness, high on task and relationships.

    b   is high on effectiveness, low on task and relationships.

    c   is high on effectiveness, high on task and relationships.

    d   is low on effectiveness, low on task and relationships.

 answer

8 Which of the following is essential for a leader:

    a   being followed?

    b   being firm?

    c   being decisive?

    d   being sympathetic?

 answer

9 Which of these is associated with the autocratic leadership style:

    a   system 1?

    b   system 2?

    c   system 3?

    d   system 4?

 answer

10   Which theorist suggested the taxonomy from System 1 to 4:

   a   Argyris?
   b   Botrytis?
   c   Likert?
   d   Maslow?

Topic 7   Motivation

1   Who do you think said 'The expenditure of physical and mental effort in work is as natural as play or rest':

   a   Rensis Likert?
   b   Abraham Maslow?
   c   Fred Herzberg?
   d   Douglas McGregor?

2   Ego needs are the need to:

   a   be able to show off your physical beauty.
   b   be able to demonstrate your strength of personality.
   c   be constantly the centre of attention.
   d   be able to be recognized for special skills.

3   Which of the following is a motivator, according to Herzberg:

   a   achievement?
   b   recognition for achievement?
   c   advancement?
   d   the job itself?

4   Which of the following is not a hygiene factor?

a air conditioning?
b growth?
c friends?
d bosses?

 *answer*

5 Job enlargement is:

    a giving more responsibility in the work.
    b adding similar tasks to fill spare time.
    c altering the job description but leaving job content alone.
    d rotating people among different jobs.

 *answer*

6 In the Lawler & Porter model, reward has a direct effect on:

    a performance.
    b effort.
    c motivation.
    d feedback.

 *answer*

7 In contingency theory, what is motivation a function of:

    a valency and expectancy?
    b valency and hygiene factors?
    c Theory X and Theory Y?
    d expectancy and probability?

 *answer*

8 Which of these most closely defines Theory X:

    a man is naturally inert?
    b man is naturally artistic?
    c man is naturally rebellious?
    d man is naturally energetic?

 *answer*

9 Basic salaries in the UK banks are not based on:

    a the grading system.
    b job evaluation.
    c the Hay/MSL scheme.
    d length of service.

10 Which of the following characterizes the reward system for most employees in the UK clearing banks:

    a payment by results?
    b payment in kind?
    c starting pay according to qualifications?
    d payment on commission?

Topic 8 Personnel practices

1 The manpower plan deals mainly with:

    a accelerated management development schemes.
    b the progress of staff through the organization.
    c the strengths and weaknesses of the staff.
    d the supply and demand for staff in the future.

2 During an appraisal interview, the appraiser should:

    a always agree with the staff member being appraised.
    b concentrate on driving home the shortcomings in performance.
    c eliminate discussion of imaginary or emotional problems.
    d actively encourage suggestions as to future responsibilities.

3 The process of recruitment should start from:

a   the job description.
b   the personnel manager's inclinations.
c   the advertisement.
d   the application form.

4   The 'halo effect' is:

a   an aura around someone's personality.
b   the rub-off effect of one personal quality on another.
c   bias in favour of a physical type.
d   a way of concealing your personality.

5   Which of these does not appear as a point in the Seven Point Plan:

a   physical attributes?
b   likely contribution?
c   domestic circumstances?
d   general intelligence?

6   Management training is best done:

a   on the job.
b   off the job.
c   externally.
d   by mixed mode.

7   'Setting training objectives, and checking before-and-after performance' is called:

a   consolidation.
b   verification.
c   validation.

d affiliation.

8 Personnel departments are normally responsible for:

    a the standard of clerical excellence.
    b staff morale at the workplace.
    c the administration of disciplinary procedures.
    d the level of literacy in the staff.

9 Appraisal intereviews should be between:

    a the staff member and the immediate superior.
    b staff member, immediate superior and manager.
    c staff member, union representative and manager.
    d staff member, branch colleagues and manager.

10 Central personnel need appraisal forms principally in order to:

    a make decisions on gradings and promotions.
    b make judgements about manager's appraisal competence.
    c apply disciplinary measures to the staff.
    d publish the findings to senior managers.

Topic 9 Groups

1 Form, storm, norm, perform concern:

    a the history of a football club.
    b the formation of a new branch.
    c the development of a group.

d the accuracy of the weather forecast.

2 A group leader is not necessarily responsible for:

a task needs.
b team needs.
c individual needs.
d domestic needs.

3 Which of the following is closest to being the expression of a group norm:

a 'you smoke too much, Patricia'?
b 'we don't usually smoke between courses, Caroline'?
c 'that's the twelfth cigarette since lunchtime, Paul'?
d 'we'd better find a smoking compartment, Brian'?

4 In Leavitt's experiments, which was the most efficient communication pattern:

a the Y formation?
b the circle?
c the chain?
d the wheel?

5 Of the following, which is false about an informal group:

a management always recognizes its importance?
b management sometimes recognizes its importance?
c management sometimes recognizes its leaders?
d management often ignores its existence?

6 'They are psychologically aware of each other': this is part of whose definition of a group:

    a Schmidt?
    b Schlemiehl?
    c Schein?
    d Schcharansky?

7 A group decision is:

    a a decision concerning the group.
    b a decision agreed by the group.
    c a decision concerning the group boundary.
    d a decision to set up a group.

8 The first thing that would happen to Lesley if she contravened the group's norms would be:

    a expulsion.
    b isolation.
    c overt rebuke.
    d tacit disapproval.

9 'Work is a group activity': this is a major conclusion from:

    a the Hierarchy Experiments.
    b the Harrad Experiments.
    c the Hawthorne Experiments.
    d the Heathcliffe Experiments.

10 The informal group leader is inevitably:

    a more powerful than the formal group leader.
    b the same person as the formal group leader.

c   less powerful than the formal group leader.
d   appointed by the informal group.

answer

Topic 10   Industrial relations

1   Collective bargaining is a system with the aim of:

a   negotiating wage settlements.
b   resolving conflict between employers and employees.
c   avoiding the need for legislation.
d   arguing about exploitation by employers.

answer

2   Which of the following represents bank staff in wage negotiations:

a   the CBU?
b   the CBI?
c   the FBI?
d   the CBS?

answer

3   The FLCBE is:

a   Federation of Local Clearing Banks Executives.
b   Federation of London Clearing Banks Executives.
c   Federation of London Clearing Banks Employers.
d   Federation of London Clearing Banks Employees.

answer

4   In which of these banks has BIFU sole negotiating rights:

a   the Royal Bank of Scotland?
b   the Bank of Ireland?
c   the National Westminster Bank?

d Barclays Bank?

5 BIFU is affiliated to:

    a the Trades Unions Council
    b the Confederation of British Industry.
    c the Labour Party.
    d the Aims for Industry Organization.

6 The Equal Pay Act relates mainly to:

    a equal pay for black and white.
    b equal pay for men and women.
    c equal pay for old and young.
    d equal pay for everyone in society.

7 The Health and Safety at Work Act was passed in:

    a 1954.
    b 1964.
    c 1974.
    d 1984.

8 You cannot normally be fairly dismissed without:

    a redundancy payments.
    b a good reference.
    c appeal to an Industrial Tribunal.
    d a written warning.

9 The clearing banks' redundancy agreement with the unions most closely:

    a is considerably more generous than the law insists on.
    b is considerably less generous than the law insists on.
    c complies exactly with what the law insists on.
    d bears no resemblance to what the law insists on.

10 On which of these have the bank employers and unions agreed to negotiate:

    a minimum level managers' salaries?
    b Xmas holiday entitlement?
    c unilateral arbitration in disputes?
    d provision of social and sporting facilities?

 Answers follow on pages 188-189. Score 2 marks for each correct answer.

Answers

Topic 1   Organizations

1d	2a	3c	4d	5a
6a	7d	8b	9c	10d

Topic 2   The banking environment

1c	2b	3a	4d	5c
6c	7b	8a	9d	10c

Topic 3   Managerial roles and processes

1a	2c	3a	4d	5b
6c	7d	8a	9c	10b

Topic 4   Managerial techniques and tools

1d	2b	3a	4d	5a
6c	7b	8d	10b	

Topic 5   Communication

1c	2b	3a	4d	5b
6a	7c	8c	9a	10d

Topic 6   Leadership

1b	2c	3c	4a	5d
6a	7b	8a	9a	10c

Topic 7   Motivation

1a	2d	3all	4b	5b
6c	7a	8a	9d	10c

Topic 8 Personnel practices

1d	2d	3a	4b	5b
6d	7c	8c	9a	10a

Topic 9 Groups

1c	2d	3b	4b	5a
6c	7b	8d	9c	10d

Topic 10 Industrial relations

1b	2a	3c	4a	5a
6b	7c	8d	9c	10a

Score Grid

Topic	Score ?/20	Revision campaign					
		Revision order 1–10	Study guide page no.	MCQs page no.	Score ?/20	Post test page no.	Score ?/20
1							
2							
3							
4							
5							
6							
7							
8							
9							
10							